JOSÉ MARÍ

MY STORY

Family, Cuba & Living
the American Dream

Primera edición, 2018

EDICIONES UNIVERSAL
P.O. Box 450353 (Shenandoah Station)
Miami, FL 33245-0353. USA
(Since 1965)

e-mail: ediciones@ediciones.com
http://www.ediciones.com

Library of Congress Control Number: 2018940921
ISBN-10: 1-59388-296-3
ISBN-13: 978-1-59388-296-9

Text preparation: María Cristina Zarraluqui

Cover design: Caroline de Lasa
Backcover design: Luis García Fresquet

MY STORY

Family, Cuba & Living
the American Dream

COLECCIÓN FÉLIX VARELA # 58

EDICIONES UNIVERSAL, Miami, Florida, 2018

To María Teresa, who thinking of our progeny encouraged me to write my memoirs, and on whose boundless support I have relied in the life we have shared together.

TABLE OF CONTENTS

APRIL 27, 2018

Dear children and grandchildren:

I am very happy to have written my memoirs, as some of you and María Teresa asked me to do. In addition to letting you know about our forebears, I wanted to have my life story, most of which I shared with María Teresa, reflect the key values, beginning with our faith, that are rooted in us.

A few words about how the memoirs were written. Javier Figueroa, María Teresa's brother, spent many hours interviewing me in Spanish and, as a historian, he asked the questions that were key to the narrative of my life. His wife, Sylvia, transcribed my answers and Javier wrote a draft of the memoirs in Spanish, including the section on the Figueroa - de Cárdenas family. Based on that draft, I then proceeded to handwrite the story in English making changes and adding tales that were not covered in the interviews. Given that I am not a computer techie, Jose spent many hours transcribing the story into a "Word" text in the computer. He also offered helpful suggestions on parts of the text, and his wife Caroline, designed the cover of the book. My niece Natalia provided very helpful final edits to the text.

I owe my thanks to a number of people who helped refresh my recollection on many things. Juan Manuel ("Gordo") Salvat, Bernabé Peña, and José Antonio González Lanuza, companions of mine in the Cuban struggle, helped me write that part of the memoirs. My sister Natalia, with her colossal memory, helped me write about our parents, siblings, our early life in Miami, and then in New Haven.

I hope you will enjoy the read.

With my love.

Papi/Abuelo

FAMILY BACKGROUND

I was born in Havana, Cuba, on November 28, 1941, in my home at calle 11, #610, between calle 6 and avenida Ramón Mendoza in Alturas de Miramar. My parents were Miguel de Lasa y Broch and Conchita Urrutibeascoa y Montalvo. And my grandparents were José María de Lasa and Natalia Broch on my father's side and Fabián de Urrutibeascoa and Dolores Montalvo, on my mother's.

The house was built by grandfather Fabián who was born at the end of the 19th century in Spain in the town of Plentzia in the province of Biscay in the autonomous community of the Basque country. His father Sebastián, a merchant marine captain who owned a large sailboat, decided to leave Spain and sailed it with his family to Havana. When he was seven years old, Fabián was sent to Pennington School, an old and very well known school in Pennington, New Jersey, for his elementary and high school education and thereafter to Princeton University. I do not know Sebastián's business in Cuba, but he must have been financially well positioned to be able to send a son to private schools in the U.S. Fabián was a skilled athlete and football player and while playing for Princeton was selected by Walter Camp, the so called "Father of Football" and the head of the Intercollegiate Athletic Association of America, for the "right end" position on the All American Football team in 1897 and 1898. However, he was denied the honor because Fabián was a Spanish citizen and Spain and the U.S. were then at war. Strangely enough, Princeton does not have a record of Fabián's attendance. Both Natalia my sister and I have copies of the Walter Camp letter, and there is a room in Princeton with photos of football teams with one showing Fabián with the nickname "Ruti," as he was known in school. If any of my grandchildren goes to Princeton, he or she should investigate the reason why Princeton expunged great grandfather Fabián from its attendance records. Following graduation, Fabián worked for three years in New York and then moved to Cuba where he became the president of a major printing company that among other items printed the country's weekly lottery tickets and mail stamps.

In Cuba, Fabián married my grandmother, Dolores Montalvo, and they had two children: my mother and Tío Andrés. I did not have much contact with Fabián and never met his wife Dolores who died relatively young. Years after her death, Fabián married Eska Carson Spier, an American lady with whom he remained married until his death in 1949. Tío Andrés worked with his father in the printing company. He was gay and loved by his family at a time and in a culture filled with prejudice against homosexuals.

My paternal grandfather José María, whom we called "Abuelo," was born in Cuba. His family owned three sugar mills in the late 19th century when Cuba was still a colony of Spain. Two small sugar mills were located in the province of Pinar del Río near a bay, which was named "Lasa Bay." A larger one was located in the province of Matanzas. These sugar mills and many others disappeared in the economic collapse resulting from the War of Independence. The war, which began in 1895 and ended in 1898 following the U.S. military intervention in Cuba at the last stages of the war, devastated Cuba and dramatically shrunk the economy, forcing many people to leave the island. Abuelo, however, stayed in Cuba, and owned a sugar plantation, called a "colonia." A "colono" was a sugar cane grower who sold the crop to a nearby sugar mill. Abuelo's colonia was in the province of Oriente, in Eastern Cuba, in the same area where, coincidentally, my maternal grandfather Fabián also had a colonia and where they met each other – little did they know that eventually they would share the same grandchildren. The sugar mill that processed the sugar cane grown by these colonias was called Chaparra. And it was there that Abuelo developed a close friendship with General Mario García Menocal, a veteran of the War of Independence who served as Cuba's president during 1917-1922, and who at the time administered the Chaparra sugar mill. Years after Menocal became the chief of the Conservative Party, Abuelo decided to run for office and was elected to the House of Representatives.

Abuelo married Natalia Broch y O'Farrill and had three children: my father Miguel, Tío José María and María Luisa ("Tía Bebita"). Natalia died in New York while giving birth to Tía Bebita. After her death, Abuelo traveled frequently spending long seasons in Paris and not quite taking good care of his children. In his old age, he came to live in our house in Havana, and lived mostly confined to his room. As a young boy, I had a great relationship with him. I always spent time with him after school, helped him prepare his delicious fruit gelatin, and rarely missed the opportunity to watch a baseball game together on TV. He died at home in his mid-eighties and was laid for viewing in the house chapel.

Abuelo had a sister named Catalina who married Pedro Estévez. At some point, she fell in love with a rich sugar farmer, Juan Pedro Baró, but could not marry him because there was no divorce law in Cuba at the time. Hers was one of the first divorces recognized in Cuba, in 1917, during the presidency of General Menocal, Abuelo's good friend – (it's always been helpful to have friends in high places). Both her house in the Vedado neighborhood of Havana and her tomb in the Colón Cemetery enjoy wide recognition for their architectural and artistic value. In fact, the Cuban government has turned her Vedado home into a tourist attraction, which the government named "Casa de la Amistad" ("House of Friendship"), and several books and articles have been written about her life. (You can search her name "Catalina Lasa" in the internet to see her photos and learn more about her life.)

My entire family and I enjoyed a very strong and enjoyable relationship with Tío José María. As a young man, he studied in Switzerland at Le Rosey International School where he was a classmate of the Shah of Iran, the last ruler of Iran before the Iranian Revolution, and Richard Helms who years later became the Director of the Central Intelligence Agency. Tío José María, like my father, had a diplomatic career and served for many years first in Washington D.C. and then at the Cuban Consulate in New York. After the Cuban Revolution, he left his diplomatic career and decided to stay in New York. For a good number of years he was employed by the American Council for Émigrés in the Professions, an organization that helped many refugees, all professionals, mostly from Communist countries, resettle in the U.S. Although he never married, he led an active social life in New York and maintained weekly contact with his family, whether in New York or in New Haven, Connecticut, where my parents lived after arriving in the U.S. in 1961. They were subsequently joined in New Haven by my sister Natalia and her four daughters: Natalia, Elena, Dolores and Cristina. Conchita Arias, the children's nanny who accompanied my sister when she left Cuba, went with them to New Haven. Natalia's husband, Adolfo Delgado, remained in Cuba in prison serving a six-year term of a 15-year sentence for having conspired against the Castro regime.

Tío José María visited us in New Haven and when María Teresa and I moved to Larchmont he visited there as well. He loved New York City dearly and would walk for miles every day after retiring to keep himself fit. He also much enjoyed visiting with his old female socialites. After becoming ill with terminal cancer and unable to live alone unassisted, my niece Cristina and Steve Olsen her husband took Tío into their home in Brooklyn and he lived there for two months. I don't think that Tío was fully aware of the seriousness of his situation and wanted to remain living in his home of many years. María Teresa and I managed to convince him to move to our apartment in Chicago for what we told him would be a temporary visit and he, kind of reluctantly, accepted the invitation. He lived with us for just a few months before he died early in 1999. Fortunately, he did not have to endure severe pains at the end of his life, and enjoyed family visits, continuing daily albeit shorter walks while in Chicago. The same day he died, his sister, Tía Bebita, also died in Miami at the nursing home where she was living. I was, of course, at Tío's funeral in Chicago and the next day flew to Miami to attend Tía's.

CUBA AND OUR CUBAN ROOTS

Cuba was discovered by Christopher Columbus in 1492. Columbus was searching for a route to India – then believed to be part of Asia – but what he unintentionally discovered was an island in the Western Hemisphere. During the next 100 years Cuba was the base for the conquest and colonization of an entire continent with its capital, Havana, which was founded in 1515, becoming for many years the strategic trade center with Spain. Spanish ships used its deep-water port to rendezvous there for the trip across the Atlantic carrying the New World treasures. Cuba has a rich culture and history that I encourage you to explore. And our family has deep roots there: The presence in Cuba of the Lasa, Montalvo and O'Farrill families dates back to the 18th century, with the Broch and Urrutibeascoa families dating back to the 19th century. María Teresa's family has even older roots in Cuba, with the first member of that family having arrived in the 16th century.

The Cuban Revolution has tried to discredit Cuba's history in many respects in the effort to exalt the importance of the Revolution. I can't forget a visit a couple of years ago to a museum in the city of Holguin in Cuba honoring General Calixto García, a major figure in the War of Independence, where a docent of the museum told me with a straight face that Cuba's independence was won upon the success of the Revolution in 1959. (By the way, Calixto García is the great grandfather of our close friend Carlos García Velez of whom you will learn more later.)

In 1959, Havana was a glittering and dynamic city. Since the early part of the 20th century, the country's economy had grown dramatically fueled by the sale of sugar to the U.S. Cuba ranked fifth in the hemisphere in per-capita income, third in life expectancy, second in per-capita ownership of automobiles and telephones, and first in the ownership of TV sets per-capita. The literacy rate was 76%, fourth highest in Latin America. Cuba was the home to nine UNESCO World Heritage Sites, almost as many of the rest of the Caribbean put together. But not all was good, since there were profound inequalities in income distribution, widespread rural poverty, racial discrimination, and corruption. The Revolution had major achievements in the total elimination of illiteracy, expansion in the reach of health care, and education. But Cubans have had to pay a painful price in lost freedoms, human right abuses, absence of a truly democratic system, and the inability to develop a market based economic system.

MY PARENTS

Before I write about my parents and siblings, I want to mention two persons who were very important to me and the rest of the family: Concha and Pepe García. Every day I remember them in my prayers, immediately following those for my father and mother, and all the rest of friends and family whom I expect to meet in heaven. Concha was born in Cuba of Spanish parents and when she was 16 years old began working as a maid in my house until we all left Cuba. She met Pepe García, a Spaniard, who worked in the house next door to ours, which then belonged to Eduardo Montalvo, a first cousin of my mother and also of my father. (Two of the eight Lasa siblings married two Montalvo siblings; and two Urrutibeascoa's married two Montalvo's – I've always have found these family relationships difficult to unravel, but you can try ...) Pepe came to work at our home and married Concha in our house chapel before I was born. Concha was like a second mother to me and Pepe was my protector at all times. After we all left Cuba, Concha and Pepe stayed in our house until the day when the Government confiscated the property. They were relocated to a small apartment in Havana where they lived for the rest of their lives. Concha died first, and my niece Natalia happily was able to visit with Pepe before he died.

Mamá and Papá met, of all places, in Lake Placid, New York, while having ice cream. A number of Cubans, including members of the Lasa and Montalvo families, would spend time in Lake Placid during the hot Cuban summer months. Mamá was fourteen years old when she fell in love with Papá. A couple of years later Papá was hit by a milk truck and in the course of his hospitalization the doctors discovered that he had tuberculosis. At that time, the only remedy for the treatment of this disease was to spend time in a sanatorium, and my father was sent to a well known one located in Asheville, North Carolina. He spent three years at this sanatorium, located in the mountains, where the treatment consisted of breathing in the fresh mountain air. My father said that his bed was rolled onto a balcony where he would sleep all night, obviously with warm blankets, and how after some winter nights, he would wake up in the morning covered in snow. My mother, who was not yet married to my father, visited him often. Interestingly, my grandmother, Dolores Montalvo, who for her time had the mind of a modern, avant-garde person, was the one who brought my young mother to visit her sweetheart in the hospital.

My father developed some important friendships at the sanatorium. One was with Father Belarmino García Feito, his roommate there, who was the pastor of a major church in Havana and who helped turn my father into a devout Catholic.

Another consequential friendship was born in the sanatorium, a friendship that had a significant impact on the lives of my parents and my own over subsequent years: Florence Eberth, another tuberculosis patient at this same sanatorium, and her husband Sherwood who was with her during this entire time. Happily, both Florence and my father were cured.

The Eberths would visit my parents in Cuba and would stay in our house. After the Revolution, my father – a diplomat – was posted in Geneva, Switzerland as one of Cuba's represent- atives at the General Agreement for Tariffs and Trade ("GATT"). When he resigned his position and defected, our house in Cuba was confiscated by the government and my parents were left with no assets or money. It was then that Florence and Sher- wood invited them to move to New Haven, where they lived, and helped my parents find a house and jobs. Later in this sto- ry, I will share how Sherwood helped me get into Yale.

Papá studied law at the University of Havana, but elect- ed to pursue a career as a diplomat and also as a stockbroker. He married Mamá on June 26, 1932, in the chapel of the *Cole- gio de Belén* where he – and I – had studied. My father loved American football and on Saturdays would listen principally to shortwave radio transmissions of the Notre Dame and Navy games. Mamá was perfectly fluent in English and taught Ameri- can History at *Instituto Edison*, a prestigious private school.

I should mention that during the government of the dic- tator Fulgencio Batista in the 1950s, Mamá worked with the underground movement against Batista, serving as one of the personal drivers of Manolo Ray, one of the principal under-ground leaders of that movement. Pablín Zamora, a Belén classmate of mine, and I visited a number of Catholic schools to organize a strike to protest the Batista dictatorship. At that time, my entire family was against Batista and in favor of the fight Fidel Castro was carrying on in the Sierra Maestra. My fa-ther, however, did not at all trust Fidel and time would prove his instincts correct.

I have very good memories growing up as boy and a teenager in Cuba. I had a very close relationship with Papá at that time, more so than with Mamá who occasionally would not allow me to go places or engage in activities that Papá would allow and she feuded with him over those decisions. To this day, I remember going on Saturdays to the Havana Yacht Club, meeting Papá for lunch, and occasionally going with him to the horse races in the afternoon. Papá taught me how to drive. He would take me fishing and bird hunting and that is why I became devoted to those sports. When I turned 15, over 60 years ago, Papá gave me my first shotgun, a pumping Re-mington 20 Gauge, now happily owned and frequently used by my grandson Edward. My brother Miguel and I were able to get our shotguns out of Cuba through an embassy. Papá's Spanish shotgun, much more valuable than ours and given to him by General Menocal, was left behind and Papá would from time to time remind us with regret of this particular oversight. This shared passion for hunting and fishing I have handed down to my sons and grandsons. My grandson Edward is a great shot and Gabriel is on his way to becoming one; I guess it's in the family genes. My son Jose quit hunting after he was given a small statue of St. Francis of Assisi by his uncle and aunt, Javier and Sylvia Figueroa, on his wedding to his wife Caroline. He placed the statue in his closet and claims that it peers at him each morning as he picks out his clothes for the day. Needless to say, all the birds we hunt are edible and shared with delighted farmworkers that accompany us on our hunts in Latin America.

I remember well my first trip to the United States when I was 11 years old. Papá, Mamá and I boarded a ferry that had daily trips between Havana and Key West. Papá brought his car for the trip and we drove the entire distance from Key West to Maine making, of course, a number of stops and visiting friends in the process. I remember well entering New York City, known to my parents but new to me, with all those tall buildings, in particular the Empire State building, the then tall policemen and the incredible traffic. What an experience!

My parents, on their way to Canada, dropped me off in Maine at the home of their friends Bob Edge and his wife who had a son around my age. Bob Edge was an editor of *Field and Stream*, the well-known hunting and fishing magazine. After spending a few days at their home, their son Robert and I were placed in a Conservation Camp for a week.

Some of the memories from Maine are still fresh in my mind. The first day at their house I went swimming at a nearby pond. Oh, my God! When I got in the water, I thought I would freeze. Imagine coming from Cuban beaches and entering a Maine pond – what a shock! In the mornings, with the temperature in the high 30s or 40s, Robert and I would go and pick berries in the garden for breakfast. I was then, (and perhaps even now), still learning English so I struggled a bit at the dinner table. Robert and I went for a couple of weeks to the Conservation Camp, and, in addition to improving my English, I won a fly-fishing competition that was reported in the local newspaper. The competition consisted of putting hoops in the water and having us cast the flies into the hoops. By the way, regrettably, and despite my newspaper fame, I never became a fly fisherman. After a few weeks of vacationing in Canada, Papá and Mamá picked me up in Maine and we all headed back to New York for a couple of days. Tío José María joined us in the car ride to Key West on our way to Cuba. Quite a trip that was!

MY SIBLINGS

Natalia ("Naty"), currently 84, about whom you will read more later, has always been a very special person in the family and dear to me. She married young in Cuba. Her husband, Adolfo Delgado, was a lawyer and public notary. (Notaries in countries following the Napoleonic Code rather than Common Law, which includes all of Europe and Latin America, are lawyers who play a key role in drafting and recording transactions.) As I mentioned earlier, Adolfo was a participant in the first significant conspiracy to overthrow the Castro Regime in the early stages of the Revolution. He was captured, along with his co-conspirators, some of whom were friends and former colleagues of Fidel Castro, and spent six years in prison.

Naty and the girls, accompanied by their nanny Conchita, went to Geneva to live with my parents. When my parents left Geneva and moved to New Haven, Naty, the girls and Conchita, went to Miami and rented a small house in Coral Gables (which Naty dubbed "Dracula" because it was kind of ugly), and where I and Fernando García Chacón, a close friend who left Cuba with me, went to live for a couple of years. Fernando and I worked with the *Directorio Revolucionario Estudiantil (DRE)* (more about this later) and Naty drove a bus for the Sacred Heart School. We all engaged in other odd jobs. I worked with a company that manufactured plantain chips, which I helped cut and fry – some of which we all sold to friends on the weekends.

In the mid-1960s Naty, her daughters and Conchita moved to New Haven to live in the house that my parents had purchased. María Teresa, our daughter Bebé and I also moved in when I enrolled at Yale. A few years later, Conchita went to Spain for a vacation and never returned having married José Ben with whom we suspect she had been corresponding and planning their marriage. Soon thereafter, they moved to Paris where José found a well-paying job as a bricklayer and Conchita worked cleaning houses. When traveling to Paris, our family would always visit with them and some of us often stayed at their house in Meudon, a Paris suburb near Versailles.

Naty moved to Miami after Mamá and Elena died. She reads a lot, visits with neighbors and friends whom she drives to church to attend Mass or to doctor appointments and helps them with other needs. Her care is extended to those in need whom she gets to know. It is noteworthy that for many years Naty has looked after a blind woman who was homeless and she found her a family with whom to live. The price charged by this family for providing a home to the blind woman has been borne over the years by Naty and a friend. After raising four gifted girls alone, all accomplished and successful professionals, Naty remains a very central figure in our extended family. And,

Naty, I will never forget the gift you made to me in Cuba of your old Chevrolet, which was the first car I owned.

Elena followed in age, and as Naty, she also attended the Sacred Heart School in Havana. As a very young boy, I shared a bedroom with her and can still remember many of our conversations and prayers before we would fall asleep. She was very outgoing, loved parties, and had a number of boyfriends. She fell in love with Estanislao ("Estany") del Valle, a neighbor, and the expectation was that they would get married. It was not to be, as God called her and she decided to become a nun in the Order of the Sacred Heart, to Estany's great disappointment. My parents asked her to wait one year before joining the Order in order to have ample time to consider her decision, which she did. During that year, she travelled, enjoyed herself, remained her vivacious self and continued to date Estany from time to time. At the end of the year, she announced that her vocation was still firm and she promptly joined the novitiate. In 1962, she professed her final vows in Rome where she had been studying and volunteered to become a missionary in South Korea.

Elena spent 15 years in South Korea, the first few years at a small convent in Chunchon next to the 38th Parallel (on the border with North Korea), and then at the Order's convent in Seoul. While at Chunchon, each day she worked in the rice fields in the mornings and in the afternoons she taught English at a school. Once a month, she and the other nuns would visit a U.S. Army base, where they watched an American movie and ate ice cream. When Papá became ill with Alzheimer's, at Mamá's request, she returned to the U.S. to provide the family additional emotional support. During those years, she lived and worked at the Convent of the Sacred Heart in Newton, Massachusetts and she chose to continue her studies obtaining a masters degree in Spanish at Middlebury College.

This was the time of the Second Vatican Council when the Catholic Church made a number of significant changes as part of its spiritual renewal and it was an occasion for Christians separated from Rome to join in search for reunion. Among the many changes, albeit small in comparison, some religious orders relaxed their rules with respect to the use of religious habits. This came somewhat as a shock to Elena, who had lived for 15 years in Korea wearing her habit, in Spartan conditions, including poor food and housing, and in the early years under the perceived threat of being overrun by the North Korean troops stationed nearby.

When I graduated from Yale Law School in 1971 and María Teresa and I moved to New York, Natalia asked Elena to obtain permission from the Order to move to New Haven for some time and help her and Mamá at home in dealing with the serious situation involving Papá's illness. After a few months in New Haven, Elena decided to leave the Convent and while her difficulty in adapting to her new life in the "modernized" convent life might have been a factor in her decision to quit that life, a more important factor was her desire to move to New Haven at a time when Papá was in his last stages of suffering from Alzheimer's disease. At that time this disease was not recognized as Alzheimer's, having been lumped in with other conditions of senile dementia. After his death in 1977, Papá's brain was examined by researchers at the Yale-New Haven Hospital and we were told that those studies contributed to appropriately identifying Alzheimer's disease.

Elena became a teacher in the public school system in a low-income neighborhood. She loved her teaching career and used to say that she had found a new vocation in it, and being part of a household that, while happy, was troubled by Papá's illness and the difficult impact it was having on Mamá. Elena moved with us to Brussels in August 1978 to help our family settle there. A couple of weeks after our own arrival, she flew in with Carlos, our newborn son, and with Jose who was in a wheelchair. Jose was suffering from a serious fungal infection in his knee and spent two months in a hospital shortly after arriving in Brussels. Carlos, in fact, became the son Elena never had. She extended her leave of absence from her school in New Haven and stayed helping us in Brussels for two years. How wonderful! We returned from Europe in 1981 and continued seeing Elena, Naty and Mamá quite often both in New Haven and in Larchmont.

In 1991, Elena was diagnosed with ovarian cancer. She continued working up until three weeks prior to her death on December 25, 1993 in the New Haven home. I spent her last night, Christmas Eve, with her, both of us sleeping on and off. She died very peacefully early on Christmas night. I always say to myself that I would like to die the way she did, peacefully, with my family, and with heaven in sight. Among her many loving acts, Elena allocated funds in her will to fund a playground gym for the children in the school where she taught.

Miguel, the third in line, was my big brother, six years older than I. He was my companion in fishing and hunting and I much loved him. He died in Lima, Peru in March 2017, after suffering from a respiratory ailment for many years. His illness, which varied in intensity over the years, only rarely prevented him from engaging in his passion for hunting and fishing, which he continued to enjoy up until the final months before his passing. He married in Cuba in 1958 to Alina Hernández Corujo and had three children: Miguel, Catalina and Juan Carlos who they raised in Lima. Miguel and Alina divorced in 1983 and Miguel married briefly once more before finding his new love, Pilar Castro Mendivil, who he married in 1993. Pilar was totally devoted to Miguel, always taking extraordinary care of him, which often was difficult, and we used to comment that Miguel was kept alive in his final years thanks to her. With Alina we have always maintained a very good relationship and enjoy seeing her often while we are in Key Biscayne, Florida.

Of Miguel's courageous role in the fight against Castro you will read more. He had a notorious student life, having been expelled from three Jesuit schools, in Cuba, the U.S. and Canada. Studying was not his cup of tea – having fun, though, was. Yet his professional life as an insurance salesman was very successful; his clients always praised him for his integrity and devotion to his work and their needs. He worked 52 years for the National Western Life Insurance Company where he was recognized for many years as "Agent of the Year," as his agency, which comprised a few other agents, produced the highest premium revenue for the company worldwide.

Miguel lived for a few years in Miami working with DRE and then moved to New York. Alina, his wife at the time, had a well-placed family in Peru and they decided to move there when Miguel began to develop his career as an insurance salesman. By the way, in choosing where to live, he said it had to be a country where hunting and fishing were readily available, something he found in Peru, a country he came to love deeply. At his funeral, during his eulogy, a friend said, "...there is no Cuban that loved Peru more or a Peruvian that loved Cuba more!!!"

Especially in his later years, Miguel became closer to God, praying and attending Mass regularly. Happily, Naty and I were able to visit Miguel a few days before he died. He was visited by a priest, confessed, received communion and his Last Rites. He was ready to die and meet his Creator. After seeing the priest, when we were together he asked a couple of people in the room to please leave us alone and then he said to me, "Gordo (his nickname for me – I was chubby as a boy), I am a little troubled by a question of faith that I'd like to mention to you. I don't quite believe the story in Genesis of Noah's Ark!" I started to laugh, as I am sure he is now laughing in heaven.

FIGUEROA-DE CARDENAS FAMILY

María Teresa's parents, Miguel Figueroa y Miranda and Hortensia de Cárdenas y Goicoechea, are descendants of families that settled in Cuba in the 16th century. The Figueroas came from Santa Cruz de Tenerife in the Canary Islands, an archipelago and autonomous community of Spain located on the Atlantic Ocean. The first member of the family to arrive in Cuba was Simón Luis de Figueroa. His son, Marcos, married Francisca Hernández de Puga, also from the Canary Islands, and their son, Marcos Luis de Figueroa y Hernández de Puga was the first Figueroa to be born in Cuba in the city of Havana on February 26, 1696. The family remained in Havana for over a century, until Francisco José de Figueroa y Hernández moved to the city of Cárdenas in the province of Matanzas and married Josefa García y Zalba in 1839. One of their children was Miguel Figueroa y García who would become a prominent lawyer and politician. He became a member of the Autonomous Liberal Party and was sent to Spain as a representative in the Spanish Parliament. His advocacy for the elimination of slavery in Cuba was crucial in the enactment by the Spanish Parliament of the law that eradicated it.

Miguel Figueroa y García married Juana María Caridad Hernández y del Junco. Their youngest son, Panchito, died of malaria, at age 16, while fighting in the Cuban War of Independence. Another son, Miguel Figueroa y Hernández, was María Teresa's grandfather. He married María Teresa Miranda y Córdova in 1906. He was a prominent lawyer, a Justice of the Cuban Supreme Court, and the famed novelist, Ernest Hemingway, was one of his clients. Miguel Figueroa y Miranda, María Teresa's father, was born in Matanzas on March 26, 1907. He occupied important diplomatic positions, including serving as the Cuban representative at the Holy See (or Vatican) and, on a later date, in the Dominican Republic. He married María Teresa's mother, Hortensia de Cárdenas y Goicoechea, on August 26, 1937. Shortly after leaving Cuba as exiles in 1961, they moved to San Juan, Puerto Rico, where he became a professor of Humanities at the University of Puerto Rico, serving for ten years. As it happens occasionally, some blessings come in disguise: Miguel used to tell us that he found in his teaching career his true vocation. He was a profoundly religious person, often telling us that we always have to be ready to accept God's will. Whether his exile was God's will or not, he certainly accepted the change. Miguel died on September 8, 1993.

On the maternal side of María Teresa's family, Bartolomé de Cárdenas arrived in Cuba in the 16th century from Granada, Andalucía, in Spain. He married Juana Ramírez Bravo on September 21, 1589. Hortensia's grandfather, Francisco de Cárdenas y Herrera, born on October 24, 1853, married María

Concepción de la Luz y Garson. One of their children, Luis Felipe de Cárdenas y de La Luz, married María Goicoechea y Díaz de la Torriente, and Hortensia was one of their daughters. Hortensia was born on February 2, 1913 and died on May 13, 1996.

BELEN AND EARLY YEARS

I spent 11 years in the *Colegio de Belén,* from first grade through high school, graduating in 1959. Frankly, I only have good memories of those years for what I learned, for some of the friends I made, the school activities I engaged in, and the friendship and teachings of some of the Jesuits with whom I was close. It was at Belén that I learned about social justice and practiced it by participating throughout the school year in programs helping people in poor neighborhoods. It was at Belén's Literary Academy that I learned how to speak in public and engage in public debates. It was in that school where I strengthened my faith through Ignatian spiritual exercises (or retreats) and engaging in apostolic work. And it was at Belén that I was encouraged to fulfill civic and patriotic duties, learned first at home following the example of my parents, which included getting involved in the fight against the dictatorship of Fulgencio Batista. Fidel Castro, a Belén alumnus, and his struggle against Batista enjoyed admiration and support in the school. Little did we suspect then into what he would turn Cuba. Happily, Belén relocated to Miami after it was forced to close, its property was confiscated, and most if not all of the Jesuits expelled from Cuba. The school in Miami is named Belén Jesuit Preparatory

School and ranks today among the top preparatory schools in Florida.

I wasn't much of a successful athlete in Belén. I played baseball and volleyball, but more often than not I found myself sitting on the bench. But I kept trying... I had many good friends over my 11 years there, including Juan Rionda, Pablín Zamora, Julian Zulueta and Arístides Martínez. Arístides sadly passed away recently. Julian and I have not seen each other since graduation, I see Juan every five years at our class reunion and Pablín I see every year in Key Biscayne during the winter, playing golf and boating together. He remains a good friend.

In my last few years at Belén, I began to develop a strong inclination to become a physician. Dr. Julio Sanguily, a family friend and prominent surgeon, owned a renowned clinic in Havana and in the summertime he used to invite me from time to time to visit the clinic and watch his surgeries. In the summertime, in the afternoons, I used to work at the office of another good friend of the family, Dr. Rafael Pedraza, an internist trained at the Sorbonne University of Paris who would allow me to help him with minor tasks such as taking blood pressure, temperature readings, and keeping blood samples duly organized. And by watching him, I learned how to administer injections, something I often did while at a training camp in the Dominican Republic. (More about this later.) Needless to say, today a teenager with no medical training would not be allowed to be employed and perform the tasks that I was involved with at that time. I could not suspect then that in a couple of years after the triumph of the Revolution, when he became the head of the government's National Tuberculosis Council, Dr. Pedraza would give me a job at the Council, where I helped examine microscopic biological samples of patients to determine the presence of tuberculosis. The Council gave me a new small automobile with official license plates and painted signs of "National Tuberculosis Council Service." At that time, I was already involved in the fight against Castro and I occasionally used the vehicle to transport propaganda, copy machines, and other items we were using in the underground.

My potential medical career was promptly frustrated after I graduated from Belén in 1959, the first year of the Revolution. I enrolled in medical school at Havana University. But I never attended my first class, having been expelled from the University, along with hundreds of other students then enrolled, for refusing to sign a document endorsing the Revolution and its communist ideology.

STRUGGLE FOR A FREE CUBA

Obviously, the Cuban Revolution has had an enormous impact on my life and our whole family. As mentioned earlier, we strongly opposed the dictatorship of Fulgencio Batista, but our enthusiasm for the Revolution waned within months of its triumph and Miguel and I became involved in the underground fight against the regime.

Around that time, I joined the *Agrupación Católica Universitaria* (ACU), a Christian life community of male university students and professionals. Felipe Rey de Castro, S.J. founded ACU in Cuba in 1932. When I entered ACU in 1960, Amando Llorente S.J. was the director and remained as its leader until his death in 2010. A saintly man, he was my spiritual director and led the annual retreats in which both María Teresa and I participated. Many ACU members had joined in the fight against Batista, and following the Revolution's embrace of communism, ACU members became leaders of the principal organizations in the fight against Castro: *Movimiento de Recuperación Revolucionaria* (MRR), DRE and *Movimiento Demócrata Cristiano* (MDC).

The mission of ACU is to form Catholic men as leaders in the propagation of the faith. Its headquarters are in Miami with other principal chapters or groups in Atlanta, Washington, D.C. and San Juan, Puerto Rico. Its members are expected to try to follow as best they can the example of Jesus, live a life centered on prayer, the sacraments, and apostolic work, strive for academic and professional excellence, and participate annually in spiritual exercises developed by St. Ignatius of Loyola, the founder of the Jesuit Order. In Cuba, many members felt the call to get involved in politics, social work, and the training of future leaders. A number of them joined the fight against the Batista dictatorship, with three members being cruelly killed in the last days of the regime. Fr. Llorente met Fidel Castro when Castro was a student at *Colegio de Belén* and became friends, a friendship that was strengthened when during a student excursion in Oriente province, Fr. Llorente fell in a river and possibly facing drowning was rescued by Castro. Later, Fr. Llorente visited him in the Sierra Maestra during the fight against Batista. Neither could imagine then that ACU would become a focal point in the fight against Castro when it became evident that he was intent on establishing a communist regime.

I joined ACU invited by Guacho González Mora who was married to Natalia Sandoval, a granddaughter of Cosme de la Torriente, a prominent Cuban patriot, politician, lawyer and statesman. When I was a boy and young teenager, I had the privilege of knowing him well, as he used to invite me often to accompany him to his farm near Havana where I learned to ride horses. He was married to Estela Broch. My grandmother, Natalia, was her sister.

At ACU, I made very good friends with whom I happily have remained close. They include Fernando García Chacón, Bernabé Peña, Luis Fernández Rocha, Juan Manuel ("Gordo") Salvat, Alberto Muller and Ernesto Fernández Travieso, a Jesuit priest who some of you know well, as he accompanied us on several family vacations. They all became leaders of DRE, which was originally formed in 1960 as a student unit of MRR called *Directorio Estudiantil* led by Luis Fernández Rocha. Shortly after its formation, Muller and Gordo Salvat, who were in Miami, returned to Cuba and DRE became independent of MRR. Muller and Luis were named Secretary Generals or co-heads of the group. It was around that time that DRE organized a protest in Havana Central Park against the visit to Cuba of Anastas Mikoyan, the First Deputy Premier of the Soviet Union, triggering the arrest of the DRE participants. I joined DRE shortly thereafter and became one its leaders. My name in the underground was Pedrito and I became heavily involved in propaganda activities and in helping coordinate various sections of the organization.

There are some anecdotes that I would like to share. One deals with the operation to help infiltrate into Cuba a group traveling from Miami carrying two tons of arms. The infiltration group included Ernesto Fernández Travieso, José Antonio González Lanuza and July Hernández. I remember that it was Holy Thursday in March 1961. As I often did, I went to San Antonio Church that day, and there met with Luis Fernández Rocha and Bernabé Peña. At some point during the service, Armando Acevedo, the DRE telegraph operator, joined us. He informed us of the expected arrival that night of the infiltration group and the arms. It was through telegraphic messages that we were in contact with people in the Miami office of the Central Intelligence Agency (CIA). The boat was to arrive at "Punto Enrique" close to a beach east of Havana. The problem was that those in DRE responsible for handling the infiltration operations were at that time in another province away from Havana. So Bernabé, Luis, Julio Hernández Rojo, and I had to do the job.

We left for Punto Enrique in two cars, with Luis and Julio in one, and Bernabé and I in the other. We crossed the tunnel in Havana Harbor, and, as we approached the tollhouse, we realized that soldiers were checking the vehicles crossing the tollhouse. Bernabé and I were armed and decided to drop our pistols out of the window. What a scare! By the way, Bernabé and I were praying the rosary while driving there, hoping for the best. When we arrived at Punto Enrique the boat was already there and close to the shore. But we encountered two problems.

First, there was a family fishing at the shore and, more problematic, we did not have the correct passwords to identify ourselves to those on the boat some 100 yards from the shore. Luis solved the first problem by approaching the family and identifying himself as "Luciano" (his name in the underground) the Secretary General of DRE, and telling them, "that boat out there is bringing arms and we must detain you." The wife of the fisherman began crying and yelling. Fortunately, we were able to calm her and, in fact, the husband ended up helping us bring in the arms, maybe out of fear of what we could do to them, although we had no intention of harming them. We, as well as the family, were all very nervous. We let the family go after the conclusion of the operation.

The other problem – that of lacking the correct signals and passwords to identify ourselves – was more troublesome. We did not have radio communication and neither were we the team in charge of assisting in these infiltrations. We started shouting at those on the boat who were actually ready to kill us thinking that we were preparing an ambush. I knew José Antonio was on the boat, so I yelled, "The Navarrete Twins." I was referring to Ana Lourdes and Julieta Navarrete who José Antonio knew well. And, thank God, that did the trick! Those words were sufficient to corroborate our identity and probably saved our lives. Then the infiltration of people and arms began. It lasted a few hours and the captain of the boat, Kikío Llansó, asked us to hurry up because there was a frigate looking for the boat, to which Bernabé answered, "We have a million soldiers looking for us!" This operation illustrates how ill prepared we were to engage in these tasks, but we had to do it.

We hid the arms taken from the boat in the mangroves, which were abundant in the area. There was no time to bury them and we had no way to transport them. The cargo included 60,000 Cuban pesos (then equivalent to U.S. dollars), which were counterfeit, and many of the bills became useless because they had gotten wet with salt water, disfiguring the bills. The money was intended to be used by Alberto Muller and the group planning a mission in Sierra Maestra, the same mountains where Castro went fighting after landing in Cuba. Government forces discovered the arms the next day and we suspect that it was the fisherman who reported the operation to the security forces, probably out of fear that the government might suspect that he was linked to the operation. It was a failed operation, as far as the arms were concerned, but we succeeded in infiltrating three key members of our group into Cuba.

Another anecdote to share involves a broadcasting plant, the approximate size of a small record player that was invented by Mario Arber who collaborated with us in the underground. Mario's plant transmitted in the Cuban television frequencies and was able to interrupt a TV broadcast, stop the voice transmissions, and interject a voice message from us. The antenna to transmit was placed on the roof of safe houses and the transmissions lasted less than one minute for fear of the authorities finding, through the process of triangulation, the location of the house where the transmission was coming from. My brother Miguel and Eddie Crews were in charge of placing and holding the antenna on the roof and passing an electrical cord connecting the antenna to the plant in a room where Mario operated it. Our message was pre-recorded and connected to the plant for the transmission. The most successful operation consisted in interrupting a speech of Fidel Castro at Havana University and interjecting our subversive voice message while Castro's image remained on the screen.

A funny, but somewhat frightening, event occurred on a rainy day that triggered a mild electric current in the antenna. Miguel and Eddie both had a stutter and the syllable most difficult to pronounce was "co." Current in Spanish is "corriente." When Miguel, who was holding the antenna on the roof far away from the room where Mario was operating the plant, started to experience the current in his hands he began alerting Eddie by stuttering loudly "co-co-co" without getting to the following syllables, and Eddie also on the roof and understanding Miguel's alarm, turned over to Mario also stammering "co-co-co." It took some 20 to 30 seconds for Mario to get the message and disconnect the plant from the electrical outlet, all during which time Miguel continued to hold the antenna still shouting the first syllable "co-co-co." We couldn't stop laughing when we heard the story! And even today, many years after it happened, some of us often recount the story when we get together, just to have a laugh.

A far more serious event occurred when Miguel almost lost his life, during an incident also involving the transmission plant, which was kept hidden in a country house owned by Miguel's father-in-law. One day Miguel was moving the plant from the country house to Havana in Mamá's small Vauxhall (a well known British automobile) when he encountered a roadblock with three soldiers intercepting passing vehicles. He could not stop and try to reverse course. So he went forward without stopping, shooting with his pistol and hitting two of the soldiers. The third one, whom he had not seen, opened fire with his machine gun. Miguel was hit in his left thigh, with the bullet passing through just a few millimeters from the femoral artery. He was bleeding and in pain but was able to continue driving until reaching a plaza with a parking area in front of the Havana Yacht Club. Stopping at a traffic light before the plaza, he saw Victor Morales, a friend of the family married to a cousin of Mamá and told him that he was bleeding, having been shot. He then went to a parking space located inside the plaza and parked the Vauxhall. Victor Morales followed him and took him in his car to the house of Fernando García Chacón, located nearby, where a tourniquet was put in his leg to control the bleeding. Later that day, a doctor treated his open wound. Miguel Figueroa, who would in a couple of years become my father-in-law, and who was a diplomat and had many contacts in the diplomatic world, was able to get Miguel to temporarily hide in the Apostolic (or papal) Mission in Havana. After hiding a few days there, he obtained political asylum[1] in the Mexican

---

[1] Following the failure of the Bay of Pigs Invasion and the subsequent repression that spawned in Cuba, hundreds of people, including Miguel and myself, sought asylum in various embassies from Latin American countries, and thereby obtained exit permits to escape Cuba. In the 19th and 20th centuries, Latin American countries suffered a number of dictatorships with frequent regime changes and ensuing governmental repressions. People often sought protection or "asylum" in foreign embassies located in those countries. Embassies offered "extraterritorial protection" to individuals invited to enter the embassies to avoid being arrested, but such individuals could not leave the embassy or the country without government permission. Latin American countries, including Cuba, entered into a treaty of "Political Asylum," under which a person who

Embassy and after four months Miguel received safe passage to leave Cuba. The bullet-ridden car was taken over to our house where Pepe the caretaker, took an axe to the various bullet holes to make it appear as if the car had been involved in an accident.

Our house in Havana was a meeting place for leaders of the resistance, both from DRE and MRR, with my sister Natalia often offering lunch. It was there where I met Rogelio González Corzo (known as "Francisco" in the underground), a member of the *Agrupación Católica Universitaria* and leader of MRR who was arrested in another house days before the April 17, 1961, Bay of Pigs invasion and promptly executed. The house of Luis Fernández Rocha was also often used as a meeting place. I remember well the meetings I held there with Luis, Bernabé, Chilo Borjas and occasionally Miguelón García Armengol, a very good friend of Miguel. Miguelón was caught, tried and condemned to death. His execution was avoided when through family connections certain foreign governments ex-erted influence to spare his life. He served a very long prison sentence.

DRE had an "Action" group that was preparing an upris-ing in the Sierra Maestra led by Alberto Muller. In cities, espe-cially Havana, the Action group's main task involved placing plastic explosives supplied by the CIA in power and telephone

---

sought asylum in an embassy for a "political cause" was entitled to leave the country, if a "safe conduct pass" (safe passage) was obtained.

lines to disrupt as much as possible the basic power and communication infrastructure of the city. These actions also served to let the local population know that a counterrevolution was in progress. The explosives were placed in locations and at times unlikely to impact passersby.

In retrospect, these activities now seem kind of crazy and had very little effect in countering the progress of the Revolution. It was a difficult and complex moment and a situation fraught with risk. Members of our group such as Virgilio Campanería and Alberto Tapia Ruano were caught and executed. Tomás Fernández Travieso, brother of Ernesto, was arrested with Virgilio and Alberto, but was not executed because he was 16 years old. He and others such as Alberto Muller, Antonio García Crews, and Miguelón, just to mention a few, went on to serve long prison sentences.

Fernando García Chacón, six years older than I, became, and remains, a very good friend. I don't remember how I met him, probably at ACU, during the conspiratorial years working together with DRE. He was a young lawyer at one of Cuba's most prominent law firms where the father of the Navarrete young ladies, good friends of ours, was a senior partner. It was through his help that I was able to hide and escape arrest and eventually obtain asylum in the Venezuelan Embassy.

The Bay of Pigs Expeditionary Force landed in Bahía de Cochinos in the province of Las Villas, on April 17, 1961. The CIA organized the invasion, working closely with the Pentagon. The members of the Brigade were trained in Guatemala and boarded ships in Nicaragua to proceed to the landing site. We in the underground knew that the invasion was being planned, but the CIA did not let us know in advance the landing date or specific plans for fears that there could be a leak that might alert the Cuban government. The goal of the underground movement was to try to incite an urban uprising to coincide with the landing. DRE had organized a force of some 1,500 fighters for an uprising in Havana. Other organizations of the underground had made similar plans for uprisings in Havana and other cities. But these plans were frustrated by our lack of knowledge of the date of the invasion and, more importantly, by the fact that we never received the arms the CIA was to send to us. The urban uprising would have been a critical compliment to the invasion force, enhancing their chances of success in the Bay of Pigs.

A more significant impact on its failure was President Kennedy's decision to stop the air attacks to destroy the Cuban air force prior to the invasion. One or two air raids did take place but he cancelled several other that were planned to follow. Kennedy, recently elected and briefed on the operation, had serious doubts about the invasion plans. However, instead of canceling the invasion, he let it go forward despite the Pentagon's belief that the full destruction of the Cuban air force was necessary for the invasion to have a chance of success. This belief was based on the fact that a swamp of dozens of square miles surrounds the Bay of Pigs with only one road providing vehicle access and air control was thus essential.

Immediately following the landing, the government began arresting thousands of people suspected of being part of the underground movement or being sympathizers, and detaining them in sports stadiums. Those of us working with DRE went into hiding. Fernando and I hid for a few days in an apartment on Fifth Avenue owned by Fernando's uncle. Fernando's sister, Teresita, used to bring us food, and one day on her way in to visit us she saw security forces surrounding the apartment building. She went to a nearby public phone (no mobile phones yet in existence) and alerted us. Looking out of a window, Fernando realized that indeed military personnel were outside. We immediately began calmly going down the stairs, and, in so doing, encountered a couple of military personnel climbing the stairs who actually told us that they were looking for some suspects and asked if we knew of someone living in the apartment we had just left. They did not ask us any questions about ourselves – how stupid of them! We said "yes," that we believed someone lived there. We exited the building, went to the corner, and got into a bus. What a fright, and again how lucky we were!

With the help of a friend of Fernando, we were able to hide in the apartment of a senior functionary of the Spanish Embassy. In a few days, through contacts of Miguel and Viruca Humara, friends of Fernando and known to me, we were granted asylum in the Venezuelan Embassy, staying a few days in the building housing its chancellery and then moving to a house in the suburbs also under the control of the Venezuelan Embassy.

We were about 100 people in the house and spent over four months living there. We were 12 in our room sleeping in cots. I was able to meet a number of prominent people, including Levi Marrero, an important historian and geographer, and Carlos Alberto Montaner who became a well-known journalist in Madrid and Miami. Mario Seigle was a physician married to María Sardiñas, a first cousin of María Teresa. I was losing weight and Mario took care of me by making sure I ate as much chocolate as possible. I also developed a friendship with María Comellas and her brother "Cawy" and enjoyed having many conversations with them.

Food was brought in daily, not in large quantity, but enough to keep us fed. Beer and rum and other beverages were also available from time to time. One day, Federico Arvesú, S.J., a priest and psychiatrist, came to visit and give us communion. I remember how his hand holding the host trembled while placing it on our tongues. He was as moved as we were. There were several married couples that took turns using a separate room to have marital relations. The days and times to use the room were drawn by lot. That was life in the house for over four months: make friends, talk, read, listen to shortwave radio, write letters, pray, sleep and dream, all in what was for such a large group a small confined space. But we were grateful to be safe.

It was a very important time in my life, most especially because it was then that I decided to declare my love to María Teresa. I had known her for a long time. Our families were good friends. Miguel Figueroa, María Teresa's father, was a neighbor of my father when they were children. I remember seeing Miguel and María Teresa's mother, Hortensia, often having dinner at our house. The grandparents Lasa and Figueroa were also friends. As a teenager, I saw María Teresa at many parties and dated her only a few times, because then I mostly dated one of the Navarrete ladies, Ana Lourdes. When I graduated from *Colegio de Belén*, I invited Ana Lourdes to be my date at my graduation party, but she became sick and couldn't make it. I decided to take my chances and went to María Teresa's home, explained to her that Ana Lourdes was sick, and asked her to be my date. She accepted my invitation! I kept dating her, but it was not until 1961 that I realized I was in love with her. I used to go daily to 5 p.m. Mass in San Antonio Church, on Fifth Avenue near her home, and my choice of church was due to the fact that it was there that I could see her even if we hardly spoke.

Father Llorente sought refuge in a house belonging to the Spanish Embassy just next to the house where we were staying. Only a fairly high cement fence separated our houses, and I began writing letters to María Teresa declaring my love for her. I would take the letters, tie them around a stone, and throw them over the fence and Fr. Llorente would then give them to Francisco ("Pancho") Miranda, a cousin of Miguel Figueroa, who frequently visited Fr. Llorente. He would then mail the letters to María Teresa in Miami. Reversing the routing of the lovers' correspondence, she would mail her responses to Pancho who would deliver them to Fr. Llorente, who in turn would pitch them to me over the fence. That is how our epistolary relationship began, which led later on, following our reunion in Miami, to our courtship, engagement, and marriage.

And Fr. Llorente's involvement in our relationship does not end in the "stone throwing" correspondence. María Teresa told me that when Fr. Llorente came to Miami, while I was still at the embassy, she went to see him and told him that although attracted to me, she felt she might have a vocation to become a nun. Fr. Llorente replied, "a nun?, maybe not; you should marry José María who is a good man in love with you and with whom I suspect you are also in love." (I suppose Fr. Llorente, being a priest who should welcome religious vocations, received a divine message that María Teresa did not really have one.) And thank God, and thanks to Fr. Llorente who married us, we have been happily married for 55 years and counting.

It was on September 9, 1961, that Fernando, others who took refuge at the Venezuelan embassy, and I were able to leave Cuba under diplomatic protection. On our short flight from Havana to Miami, I was overcome by many emotions. I was happy to be alive and escaping prison, but sad for the failure of our attempt to overthrow the communist regime, all the while knowing that some of my friends and fellow fighters were in prison or had been shot. My joy in knowing that I would soon see María Teresa again also evoked strong emotions during the flight.

Cuba had made an exception to the rule that we had to leave via the country that had granted us asylum, in our case Venezuela, and those of us who wanted to fly to Miami directly were allowed to do so. At that time people used to travel elegantly dressed. Fernando, always a very elegant man, had asked a tailor to come to the Venezuelan Embassy, take measurements, and make two suits, one for me and the other for him. We were transported to the airport on buses with police escorts and taken directly to the aircraft, for a chartered flight of Pan American Airways, then one of the largest U.S. airlines.

María Teresa and I were married on November 23, 1963, one day after the assassination of President John F. Kennedy, in the Church of the Little Flower, in Coral Gables. Fr. Llorente, of course, married us. Fernando drove María Teresa and her father to the church and he drove María Teresa and me after our wedding to Dracula for an intimate family celebration. The photos were taken in the garden of the house right across the street from Dracula, since it was much prettier. The honeymoon destination was New Orleans where we traveled in a VW Beetle that Fernando loaned me the money to purchase new for what I think was about $1,600. After a two-week honeymoon, we returned to Miami and rented an apartment on Menores Street in Coral Gables.

Naty, her children and Conchita (the nanny) moved to Miami in November 1961, at first staying with Alina, Miguel's wife, in a small apartment on 16th Street and 36th Avenue. In a few weeks, when Miguel was able to leave Cuba and came to

Miami, Naty found a house ("Dracula") at 916 Obispo in Coral Gables. She moved there with her children and Conchita. Fernando and I also ended up living there.

Dracula played a role in the fight against Castro, which continued from Miami. We used its garage to keep arms, including a 20mm cannon which we used to call Mamerto (a proper name in Spanish with mixed meanings) and which was used in DRE's attack on the hotel Rosita de Hornedo on the Havana shore where Russian military personnel were staying. (More on that later.) One day, Mr. Tower, the realtor managing the property, told us that the owners wanted to visit the house. Naty told Fernando and me to leave the house, that she would take care of the visit, and that she was praying for it to go well. After the owners inspected the house, they visited the garage where Mamerto and other arms were hidden under a large cover. Being asked what was under the cover, Naty told them that it was special machinery to be used by the Okeelanta Sugar Mill in Belle Glade, near Lake Okeechobee. This must have sounded very credible as the owners didn't ask any more questions and left the house satisfied, telling Naty they were happy she was taking such good care of it. I guess her prayers worked!

On another day, we had a fire in the house, which began in the room used by her and the girls and was due to some electrical cables in bad state that started a fire in the beds. Happily, it turned out not to be a big deal and several buckets of water took care of rapidly extinguishing the fire. Had we believed that the situation warranted a call to the firehouse, we would of course had done it. Mindful of what was in the garage, we were happy that call never took place. While we were aware that keeping arms in the garage was probably a violation of some local law, we felt somewhat protected because we enjoyed the support of the CIA, a supposition that fortunately was never tested.

With our arrival in Miami, in exile, our commitment to continue the fight remained very strong. Luis Fernández Rocha, Gordo Salvat, Chilo, Bernabé, Ernesto, José Antonio González Lanuza, and many other companions, were already in Miami. We reorganized DRE and started working to reach our objectives. Key financial support for us came from the CIA but they wanted us to concentrate our efforts in dissemination of information through the media and visits to student organizations in Latin America. I was the editor of a publication named *Trinchera* (Trench) where I wrote a column called "Frentes" (Fronts). We also had a radio program transmitted through a station in Miami, and a shortwave radio transmission from New York, with which I was also involved. Notably, DRE also established delegations and branches in a number of Latin American countries to spread our message and information.

Conflicts with the CIA began to occur early on. The CIA insisted that our operations be limited to various publications, radio broadcasts, and networking with student groups in Latin America, all activities which the CIA was financing. But we wanted to conduct the infiltration of arms to people in Cuba still working in the underground. While the CIA permitted some people infiltrating into Cuba, they did so only to gather intelligence, not to conduct any sabotage or military activities. We firmly believed that to obtain a regime change, insurrectional activities were essential and we often ignored CIA directives. As our relationship with the CIA continued to deteriorate, we began thinking of strategies to raise funds and begin independent military operations, culminating in the establishment of a training camp on Catalina Island, in the Dominican Republic. (More on this later.)

The financial support of the CIA permitted us to provide a monthly allowance to the members of DRE working in exile, principally in Miami. The allocation to each individual was determined not by the CIA but by us. Those of us on the executive committee were not paid higher than the rest. The allowances were based on need. My recollection is that my monthly allowance was around $200, increased to $300 after marriage. The CIA money was used to finance our operations, including the maintenance of a few offices in Latin America, and some military activities that we did not report to the CIA.

I was the one who signed the rental agreement for an office in Miami where we made a number of alterations, such as building partitions for offices, which we felt necessary and believed enhanced the value of the property. We had not read the agreement in detail. And the partitions were put in without asking for permission from the landlord who, upon visiting and viewing what we had done, brought a lawsuit claiming damages. I was the named defendant, since I had signed the lease. I was very nervous at the court hearing, and when addressing the judge to explain what we had done, I addressed him saying "Your highness" instead of "Your honor." The judge, the landlord, the people in the court, and the visitors who would spend their afternoons watching court hearings for entertainment, all exploded laughing. When calm was restored, the judge told the landlord that he was sorry to let him know that his case against us had to be dismissed, because the agreement was invalid since I was a minor. We of course welcomed the decision, but regretted that we had made changes in the premises without first asking permission. We approached the landlord very amicably, and while not giving him a penny, as we firmly believed that we had improved the value of the premises, we did manage to make peace.

In January 1962, a few months after arriving in Miami, Gordo Salvat, Ernesto, Fernando and I were presented with the opportunity of traveling to Punta del Este, Uruguay, to attend a meeting of the Organization of American States ("OAS"). At this meeting, foreign ministers of all the countries members of the OAS were to decide whether to expel Cuba from the OAS, given that Cuba had declared itself a communist country in violation of the norms of the OAS. The meeting took place on January 31, 1962. At that time DRE was part of the *Consejo* (Council) *Revolucionario Cubano*, an organization of Cuban exiles representing the principal parties or groups opposed to the Castro regime. Before reaching Punta del Este, Fernando, Ernesto and I went to Lima, Peru, with the objective of meeting with the president of Peru, Manuel Prado. We were able to have access to Mr. Prado through a good friend of Mr. Prado who had served as Peru's representative at the Vatican during World War II. María Teresa's father, Miguel Figueroa, became a good friend of this person while serving as Cuba's representative at the Vatican. I remember, with some embarrassment, that in the meeting with Mr. Prado, I asked him, "Mr. President, in your opinion, how does Peru propose to vote at the meeting in Punta del Este." Obviously implying that he could not answer, he responded, "Son, my opinion, personal or not, is the opinion of Peru." I excused myself – Oh! Still so much to learn... Peru voted to expel Cuba.

From Lima we traveled to Santiago de Chile where we were not very successful since most students then sympathized with Fidel Castro and did not really know who we were. We had to explain that we had all supported Castro in the fight against the Batista dictatorship, but turned against him and his regime when we realized, as Castro himself did eventually proclaim, that they were communists. From Chile we traveled to Buenos Aires, Argentina, where we really didn't have any activities on our agenda other than enjoying for a couple of days a beautiful city with good food. I recalled having gone a couple of times to the Palacio de las Papas Fritas (the Palace of the French Fries), where for $4 we could have a large and very good piece of beef and french fries and $1 for a glass of wine.

From Buenos Aires we went on to Punta del Este and met with Gordo Salvat and other DRE members who had arrived there separately. We all joined the delegation of Cuban exiles led by José Miró Cardona, a renowned Cuban lawyer who Castro appointed as prime minister early on in his revolutionary government. Miró was a good friend of Miguel Figueroa. Miró's speech was much applauded by the foreign ministers attending the conference who voted to expel Cuba from the OAS. Richard Goodwin, a friend and eventual biographer of President Kennedy, was the head of the U.S. delegation and I had the opportunity to meet him. Goodwin and other U.S. officials exerted much influence in persuading a couple of countries, Haiti in particular, in voting to expel. It was rumored that the process involved the approval of grants or other actions the countries in question were negotiating with the U.S. Following the conclusion of the meeting, we travelled around the country giving speeches denouncing the implantation of a communist regime in Cuba. Thousands of Uruguayans attended the rally that was held in the Plaza Independiente, the most important square in the capital, Montevideo.

Upon my return to Miami, I was put in charge of DRE's publicity and public information function including the journal *Trinchera*. José Antonio González Lanuza published an independent newsletter called The Cuban Report, which was sent to the U.S. media and to members of Congress. This publication played a key role in the weeks before the October 1962, Cuban Missile Crisis, a 13-day confrontation between the U.S. and the Soviet Union following the discovery of the deployment of nuclear missiles in Cuba. The discovery was based initially on intelligence gathered by the underground in Cuba and confirmed by U.S. intelligence aircraft flying over the island. The Cuban Report stressed the presence of those missiles and some members of Congress, led by the New York senator Kenneth Keating, began campaigning for a U.S. military response to remove the nuclear missiles. Following a naval blockade, and, as a result of negotiations between the regime of Nikita Khrushchev and the Kennedy administration, the Soviet Union removed the missiles from Cuba.

Around that time, I was appointed the DRE's representative to the *Consejo Revolucionario Cubano* headed by José Miró Cardona, which comprised the leading organizations involved in the fight against Castro. We had only reluctantly joined the Consejo, which we viewed as too pliable to the wishes of the CIA, and comprising traditional political groups inconsistent with our wish to remain as autonomous as possible. Our desire for autonomy followed the example given to us by other Cuban university student groups engaged in fighting the previous dictatorships of Fulgencio Batista and Gerardo Machado. A few months after joining, we indeed found that there was much politicking among its members and we terminated our relationship with the Consejo. This was hard for Miró to accept, since he had much appreciation for the work we were doing and our departure weakened the Consejo and his own role as leader. I know that our decision to exit the Consejo was also a disappointment for Miguel Figueroa given his close friendship with Miró.

Another controversial decision we took at that time was not to support the negotiations between Castro and the Kennedy administration to obtain the release of 1,137 members of the 2506 Brigade made prisoners following their landing in the Bay of Pigs invasion. Long prison sentences were imposed on them, but each prisoner had a price that would trigger a release. DRE believed that, at that moment, it was not right to engage in a negotiation with the dictatorship to engage in a trade or exchange, especially since it would not cover thousands of other prisoners who were not part of the expeditionary force but were in prison for counterrevolutionary activities. We explained and defended our criteria through the media. While I was opposed to a ransom, with the passing of time and mindful that our fight ended in a couple of years without success, I concluded that we had made an error, which I regret. Fortunately, the release of the prisoners took place after a few weeks of negotiations to pay a ransom of approximately $53 million in food and medical supplies donated by companies from all over the U.S.

Following our withdrawal from the Consejo, we continued our operations, including infiltrating people into Cuba. Luis Fernández Rocha was infiltrated in June, 1962 in an attempt to reorganize the DRE's underground movement. His efforts did not succeed, for some key members of the group had been turned in to the security forces by one of its agents who had joined the group. Happily, Luis was able to escape Cuba that September.

A significant operation DRE carried out in August 1962, involved the attack on the hotel Rosita de Hornedo, on the shore of Havana, where Soviet personnel involved in setting up the nuclear missiles in Cuba were being housed. The vessel used was a 28-foot used Bertram we had purchased. The boat shipped from Marathon Key in Florida (130 miles from Havana) and after spraying the hotel with bullets (principally using Mamerto) safely returned home. For us it was a huge publicity success, since the operation was widely covered by the media in the U.S. and the world, especially after Nikita Khrushchev, the leader of the Soviet Union, publicly accused the U.S. of having been involved in the attack.

Chilo Borjas, the head of DRE's military operations, Bernabé and I went to New York two or three days after the attack to speak with the media. Bernabé and Chilo, both participants in the raid, were invited to have dinner with Larry Spivak, co-founder and host of the prestigious public affairs program "Meet the Press," and Chilo was interviewed the next morning on the program. José Antonio González Lanuza who was in New York, and had been involved in establishing our media contacts, was interviewed on TV the day after the attack by Walter Cronkite on CBS and he also appeared on NBC. While in New York, I received a call requesting that I fly to Washington to meet with Richard Helms, then the CIA's Deputy Director whom I had met earlier through Tío José María, a classmate of Helms at Le Rosey, in Switzerland. Our meeting was not a friendly one, since we carried out the attack on the Rosita de Hornedo without coordination with or approval by the CIA. The CIA's financial support to DRE was drastically reduced and we had to suspend some of our activities, including the publication of *Trinchera*. The CIA's displeasure extended to even limiting the physical movement of some DRE members, including Gordo Salvat and Bernabé. DRE's attack on the Rosita de Hornedo and the campaign we mounted to publicize the presence in Cuba of Soviet missiles hightened the concern of the CIA with respect to DRE and its activities. Ted Shackley, CIA's station chief in Miami, wanted to cut off completely the Agency's funding of DRE, and he viewed us as volatile and hard to control.[2] But Richard Helms overruled Shackley's decision, as "Helms admired the DRE's style."[3] DRE was considered to be the most effective group involved in the fight against the Castro regime and its funding was the highest of all Cuban exile groups.

In 1963, DRE decided to engage in an action plan, the core of which was a "maritime guerilla." To put in practice that strategy two goals were key. One was to obtain financial support, beyond what still remained available through the CIA. The other key goal was to have a base of operations out-

---

[2] Shackley, Ted, Spymaster. My Life in the CIA : Dulles, Virginia, Potomac Books, Inc., p. 49.

[3] Morley, Jefferson, Our Man in Mexico: Winston Scott and the Hidden History of the CIA, University Press of Kansas, p. 163. DRE is mentioned often in pp. 129-246.

side the U.S. and near Cuba. We were able to raise enough funds from private contributions and fundraising events, which allowed us to acquire an old, but still floating, PT boat. We were able to establish a good relationship with top military officers in the Dominican Republic who permitted us to establish a base on Catalina Island, a few miles off the town of La Romana. Many years after, Casa de Campo Resort & Villas, with its famous golf courses, was established near La Romana. Little did I know that over 50 years after coming to Catalina Island as a freedom fighter, I would be back on two occasions with some of my children and grandchildren for a beach day. C'est la vie ...

We were about a dozen in the DRE's group, which went to Catalina Island, including Chilo, Bernabé, and myself. We all arrived over a period of a few days following different routes from Miami. It was July 1964. We were trying not to raise the suspicion of the CIA. I will never forget my own means of transportation in a small aircraft with a pilot who volunteered to take me, flying out from Fort Lauderdale. The pilot couldn't have been more accomplished, having been a captain in Cubana de Aviación, the Cuban airline. We stopped to refuel in the Turks and Caicos Islands, now a famous beach resort. From there we flew directly to Catalina Island. The landing was unforgettable, for the landing strip was a field of overgrown grasses, which started flying around as soon as the engine blades hit them. The aircraft was covered in green and I don't believe I had time to say a Hail Mary before the aircraft stopped. I was really scared. I was one of the first in the group to arrive. A couple of days later, Bernabé arrived from Puerto Rico in our Bertram boat.

I had married María Teresa a few months before going to Catalina Island. When I decided to join the group going to the base, María Teresa was pregnant with our first child, Bebé, and the decision to leave her was painful. I arrived at my decision during a retreat given by Fr. Llorente. María Teresa and I had discussed my wish to volunteer to go to the training camp and she agreed, however difficult that was for her. The date of my departure was not known. I was notified of it only hours before. At that time, María Teresa was attending a three-day retreat also given by Fr. Llorente. I chose not to call her with the news of my imminent departure in the middle of the retreat. Instead, I called Fr. Llorente and asked him to break the news to her that I had departed after the conclusion of the retreat. Her parents became very upset and María Teresa told them that she supported my decision and that she was very proud of me.

Life in the training camp consisted of an early run, which as then a heavy smoker I was only barely able to complete, followed by a day with training. It involved thoroughly learning the PT boat and its engines, navigation classes, the positions each of us were assigned to assume and several drills in the event of having to abandon ship. The ship was armed with a 20mm cannon (I don't remember if it was Mamerto) set in the stern and three 50-caliber machine guns, one set in the bow and the other two in port and starboard, respectively. We read and discussed books and before dinner we prayed the rosary. There was ample time to talk and have fun at the nice beach next to the huts where we slept in cots. Chilo Borjas was the chief of the base. I was in charge of the camp discipline (whatever that meant), and of the discussions on DRE's ideology. Leading the daily rosary was also on my job description. I also was the nurse for the camp. More often than not, my practice area involved giving antibiotic injections to a couple of the Dominican soldiers living on the island and afflicted by infections that I rather not describe here.

Once a week we had to practice shooting with the four guns, which we typically did at night, using tracing bullets. As you know, I am hard of hearing, which I believe was partly caused by all the sport shooting I have done, and these practice shootings from the PT boat, all without wearing earplugs. How ignorant and foolish was I in not wearing them.

My brother Miguel was stationed in Santo Domingo, the capital of the Dominican Republic, and was in contact with the air force officers who had jurisdiction over Catalina Island. It was an important position, because those officers played a key role in allowing us to use the island as a base and in supplying us with arms and ammunition. A key person who helped us in the Dominican Republic was Frank Varona who lived in Santo Domingo and was in charge of a tobacco factory. It was Frank who put us in contact with the officers in the Dominican Air

Force who permitted us to establish the base, and helped us maintain a strong relationship with them.

Some of these officers would often bring Miguel to spend the day with us on the island, flying for less than 15 minutes in their World War II fighter planes, which were the core of the Dominican Air Force. Occasionally, they would bring a large number of paloma Torcaza (pigeons of the mourning dove family) that we would enjoy eating and that had been shot in bird shoots in which Miguel and the officers often engaged. Miguel would also bring our correspondence and pick up our letters to be sent to the U.S. I wrote to María Teresa at least once a week.

Many of our non-military supplies came from Mayaguez, in the west coast of Puerto Rico. Our Bertram made the approximately 80-mile trip there from time to time. Those trips were our only means of bringing DRE visitors to Catalina Island. I was able to join Chilo in one of those trips. We left very early in the morning and headed east to cross the Mona Passage, a strait that separates the Dominican Republic from Mona Island close to Mayaguez and that is an important shipping route between the Atlantic Ocean and the Panama Canal. The passage is a difficult one for small vessels. Winds often exceed thirty knots and seas with 10 to 15 foot waves. It was on one of those days that we made the crossing. What an adventure! Chilo was a great captain and the 28-foot Bertram couldn't have behaved better as the very seaworthy vessel it is. We arrived in Mona Island in the early afternoon and anchored there for a few hours, since we had to reach Puerto Rico undetected at night. My mission for this trip, other than being Chilo's crew on the boat, was to land in Mayaguez, find a phone, and call María Teresa. And happily my mission was accomplished. Our sail back to Catalina, on the boat filled with supplies, was so easy and wonderful, in very calm seas and a night filled with stars and, of course, enjoying the success of the trip.

As mentioned before, our training on Catalina Island was designed to engage in operations to disrupt Cuban navigation. Our plans were to attack, firing from the PT boat, lighthouses in the Oriente province in eastern Cuba. We also had made plans to attack merchant vessels from the Soviet Union bringing arms to Cuba. But the plans were not executed. We never fired a single shot at one of our planned targets. Now that I am much older than I was then, I feel happy that our plans were frustrated. First of all, even if we had been successful, our actions would not have caused any appreciable damage to the Revolution, and, in a way, more significant, our failure meant that no innocent people lost their lives.

One day in September 1963, several of the officers of the air force who had been helping us flew to Catalina Island and informed us that we had to abandon the base immediately, due to pressure put on the Dominican government by the United States. President Lyndon Johnson, who was running for reelection and who was under pressure from the ongoing Vietnam War, did not want any noise to erupt in the Caribbean. One way or another, the CIA had a pretty good idea of the types of actions we were planning. The possibility that a group of Cuban Americans, who would be linked to the CIA, even if our operations were not sponsored by it, could end up attacking a vessel from the Soviet Union, was something that President Johnson had to avoid. The Dominican government had no choice, as it could not run the risk of damaging its relationship with the U.S.

Within a few hours of being asked to leave the base we were on our way to Santo Domingo on the PT boat with our arms concealed. We couldn't take the Bertram, which was broken. After a few months we were able to return it to the U.S. We docked the PT boat in the Ozama river, under the Duarte Bridge, in the middle of the Capital City hoping to recover it later. Some in our group remained in the boat, but most of us began the return to Miami. I was lucky to have been invited to stay in the home of Frank Varona. I still remember taking my first shower in almost four months, since at the base what we did was to go swimming and then spray ourselves with fresh water from a bucket. I also recall sitting at an elegant dining room table with Frank and his wife Esperanza Bravo (to this day a friend of Gordo Salvat) and enjoying a wonderful meal followed by many hours sleeping in a real bed. After a couple of days, I joined Bernabé in the La Salle School where we stayed a few days before flying to Miami.

NEW PERIOD IN MY LIFE

It dawned on me that I had to start thinking of my wife, a baby soon to arrive, our future as a family, and continue studying. Before going to the base in Catalina Island I had begun taking a few night courses at the Miami Dade Junior College in Miami. Founded in 1959 as a junior college, it is today one of the largest regional colleges in the U.S. but back then it had the nickname of "Chicken Coop College," because its original home consisted of barracks in an old naval air station. While I did pretty well in the courses I took, my main goal was to improve my English, a language that I began learning while at the *Colegio de Belén* in Havana.

As the activities of DRE started to diminish considerably, I began concentrating on studying while continuing to work delivering the Miami Herald in the Miami Northeast very early in the mornings and also working at National Food Company frying banana chips. I no longer had financial support from the CIA. Our daughter and oldest child, Bebé, was born December 21, 1964. Around that time, I contacted my parents who resided in New Haven and asked them if María Teresa, Bebé and I could go to New Haven and live with them. They agreed despite the fact that Naty, her four girls, and Conchita, the nanny, were already living in the house. I told them I intended to go to college and there were several well-known in New Haven – New Haven College, Southern Connecticut State University, and, of course, Yale.

We all knew that Sherwood Eberth, my parents' good friend, was a Yale graduate who had remained active in alumni affairs and knew some important people in the Yale administration. By this time, Naty had written from Miami a letter to Kingman Brewster, the president of Yale, recommending me, pointing out that following my graduation from *Colegio de Belén*, I had applied and been admitted to Harvard. It was already February 1965, and the admissions process, except for a few cases, was over. Sherwood managed to obtain an interview for me with the dean of Yale College and the Dean of Admissions. I couldn't believe it. I jumped on a plane and headed for New Haven. Sherwood suggested that my mother accompany me at least to be introduced to the first dean I was to interview. We all guessed that Sherwood felt that the presence of this distinguished and pretty Cuban lady could perhaps favorably impact my chances. My high school grades were first-rate and the grades in the courses at Miami Dade Junior College were all A's – but the deans could not find the name of the college in the list of accredited junior colleges. During the interview, I took full advantage to highlight my unusual background, including having been a freedom fighter, participating in radio programs including New York shortwave radio transmissions, directing the *Trinchera* Journal, and on and on. I met with the Dean of

74

Yale College first and then the Dean of Admissions, who at the end of my interview just told me "You will be admitted to Yale in the Class of 1968". While he assured me of that, he also told me it would not be official until the admissions committee so ruled.

My first stop after the meetings was at a phone booth where I called María Teresa who found it difficult to believe what had just transpired. At the end of March, I received the official Yale letter informing me that I had been admitted with a significant scholarship as a sophomore, not as a freshman. The Dean had mentioned this possibility, since I was five years older than students entering as freshmen. Also, I had five years of high school, as is typical in many countries, and had taken a few college-level courses in Miami.

Before going to New Haven for the interviews, I felt I needed to practice my English. I called Carlitos García Vélez to help me. He is perfectly fluent in English and had available a small one-bedroom apartment in Key West. Carlitos, his wife Betty, María Teresa and I got into the VW bug (I don't remember whether it was theirs or ours) and off we went to Key West speaking English. María Teresa and I had sleeping bags and we put them outside the only bedroom, which had an air conditioner, in order to get a little cool air from underneath the door. They had invited us to sleep in their room, but we demurred. It was so hot that in a few minutes we knocked on the door and took our sleeping bags into the bedroom to sleep there. The deal was not to speak a word in Spanish – only English could be spoken. Carlitos gave me one important piece of advice: He told me that at the end of my meetings, I should look into the eyes of the deans and say to them, "It has been a privilege to meet you." Good advice to keep in mind for use on special occasions.

As soon as the Yale letter arrived, we began to get ready for our move to New Haven. I went to the DRE offices to say goodbye. People there were already making plans to move on with their lives. Some of my best friends to this day are DRE companions, including Bernabé, Gordo Salvat, Ernesto, José Antonio, Alberto Muller and Luis Fernández Rocha. My close friendship with Fernando predates the DRE period. We piled the VW up to the last inch with luggage, a crib and baby bassinet, among other items. And filled with excitement, I began my non-stop drive from Miami to New Haven. Two days later, María Teresa and seven-month old Bebé flew to New York where I was happily waiting to drive them home. It was August 1965.

The house, at 240 Washington Avenue in Hamden (adjacent to New Haven), was small but with enough space to accommodate 10 people and a cat. We grew to 12 with the arrival of our sons Jose and Andrés. There were three bedrooms, which were occupied by Mamá and Papá, Naty and Conchita, and María Teresa and me. The four girls at first shared bunk beds in another room. Bebé, Jose and Andrés, one after another, slept in our room. María Teresa and I spent six years living there, three while in college and another three while in law school. When María Teresa became pregnant with Andrés, she went crying to see my mother given the limited space in the house, and my mother's memorable answer was, "Don't worry, there are many drawers in this house." I built a small office in the basement where I studied and typed my papers.

All adults in the house worked. Mamá and Naty worked at the prestigious Foote School in New Haven. Papá worked at the Yale Alumni Fund, but he had to quit when his Alzheimer's disease (not yet known as such at the time) became more acute. María Teresa was employed at the Yale Art Gallery as an assistant in a program focused on Latin America Art. Conchita worked at the house and took care of the children. I studied but was able to bring in some money teaching Spanish part-time to Connecticut State troopers at the New Haven College, as well as an extension course at the submarine base in New London, Connecticut. In my junior and senior years, I became the Junior and Senior Manager, respectively, of the Yale Birthday Cake Agency.

All students with scholarships had to work at one of the various Yale student agencies. At the Yale Birthday Cake Agency, we were given a list of all college students with their birth dates and parents' addresses. We wrote a letter to the parents inviting them to buy a cake for their son's birthday, which we delivered to the residential colleges. Most parents would order the cakes from us. The cakes were baked at the Culinary Institute of America (also known as the CIA), which was then located in New Haven. Little did I know that my relationship with the CIA had not ended. It occurred to us to give parents the option of baking into the cake a number of dimes corresponding to the student's age and, of course, adjusting the price accordingly. But we had to stop the practice when one student inadvertently ate a couple of dimes and protested.

As I am sure is still the case in many colleges, Yale had a curriculum that included "distributional requirements," which applied to me in my sophomore year. I had to take a course in calculus or in a foreign language, taught in that language. I had difficulty in algebra so calculus was not an attractive choice. I proposed taking English as it would give me an opportunity to improve my English. Shame on Yale: the Dean told me that English was not a foreign language. And I responded that it was for me. This mistake by the Yale administration turned out to be a panacea for me, because it allowed me to elect to take Spanish.

The Spanish class consisted of some 10 or 12 students. My first professor was not a native speaker of Spanish and he felt somewhat uncomfortable having me in his class. He went to the Dean and told him to move me to another class with a professor who was a native speaker. And, lo and behold, I was then enrolled for one year in another Spanish class where I sat next to George W. Bush, who would one day become the president of the United States. Years later, I remember calling him in Texas asking for money on behalf of the Yale Alumni Fund. With the passing of time he went on to become the Governor of Texas and then President. I saw him a couple of times while he was President, including at the White House where he had invited the class of 1968 to begin its 35th class reunion in 2003. Whenever I saw him he would say, "José, why in the hell did you take Spanish?" and I would respond, "Mr. President, the other choice was calculus." "Oh . . . I understand," he would say. By the way, I remember him as a warm person, often putting his arm around the shoulder of a friend, something not very common among students at that time.

In my junior and senior year I was admitted into an honors program in a divisional major known as Political Science and Economics, Division II. We were 11 students and took only one course per year in economics. The rest of the work was to read hundreds of books, write a weekly paper, and discuss it with a professor assigned to us with subject matter expertise. The first assignment was to read *The Republic* by Plato and *The Prince* by Machiavelli and compare them. The papers had to be short and I wrote a two-page paper. I got it back with most of it crossed out and three sentences left. My professor told me, "José, this is all you wanted to say." And I began learning not only to write, but to think as well. Other than the book or books assigned for our weekly papers, we had to read many others and the choice of which to read was ours. It was a stellar and varied reading list, including titles like *Che Guevara's Diary*, and *An American Dilemma*, a 1944 study of race relations authored by the Swedish Nobel laureate economist, Gunnar Myrdal. The professors kept telling us that we should read some of the books again after leaving college. As we read, we were encouraged to visit with and discuss the books with our professors.

How fabulous this was! There was only one exam per year taken at the end of the year. The grade of the senior year exam was the final grade for the two years. We all did well and our admission to graduate or professional school was based principally on the recommendations or our professors. Our professors and the honors program were well known in the major universities in the country. As a result, I was admitted both at Yale and Harvard law schools, the only ones to which I had applied.

My social life in college was very limited. I was married, with children, lived in a house with my parents, and had many jobs. Almost the only contact I had with the school and other students was in class. I was obliged to have lunch in my college, Timothy Dwight, at least once a week. But I never joined classmates for dinner or a beer. I had just a few, but very good, friends in college, in particular Merritt Fox and David Marks. David helped me with my studies both in college and at the Yale Law School. He sadly passed away at a relatively young age years ago. Years after graduation, Merritt married my niece Natalia and has remained a close friend.

While I was at Yale, we were lucky to have developed a close friendship with Alfonso and Gloria Esguerra, a married couple from Colombia. Alfonso was studying medicine at Yale. They lived close by and they became friends of the whole family. Their baby daughter, Beatriz, was about the same age as Bebé. We often had lunch or dinner together in our house or theirs and shared many other enjoyable occasions. They have remained friends to this day, and we see them during their travels to New York. We have also visited them in Bogotá.

A very sad and difficult time we all lived through was my father's illness with Alzheimer's disease. At the time, Alzheimer's was not really known, nor had it been recognized as an illness separate from other cases of senile (old age) dementia. Papá became increasingly confused and disoriented with progressive loss of memory. Before his death in 1977, for about a year he was bedridden and developed back sores. It was very sad to see him in such a condition. Towards the end, Naty and I decided to visit nursing homes with the idea of putting Papá in one and relieving the pressure his illness was creating in the house, especially on Mamá and Naty, and also on Elena when she came to live at home. They took care of his sores, bathing him, and so forth. When we came home and told Mamá that we had found a nursing home for Papá, she looked at us reproachfully and simply said, "Over my dead body will your father be moved out of this house."

When Papá had to quit his job, I went to see the head of the financial aid office at Yale to explain the situation. I told him that I was planning on taking a year off from school to work and provide financial help at the house. He smiled and said, "José, I think you are crazy. You're going to keep studying and we'll take care of increasing your financial aid." I left his office with tears in my eyes. A couple of years later, Jose, who was about two years old, developed a hernia and needed surgery. He was operated at Yale-New Haven Hospital and the bill was $800. I went again to the financial aid office and requested a loan to pay off the bill and I was told not to worry, simply to send the bill to them and they would handle it.

During my college years, I remained informed about – and saddened with – what was going on in Cuba. I corresponded frequently with some of my DRE friends and with Fr. Llorente, who visited us in New Haven on a couple of occasions. I tried to attend a spiritual retreat almost every year, most of which he directed. The frequent visits of Tío José María, who would come from New York, arriving Friday and leaving on Sunday, were very enjoyable occasions. He was quite a socialite, a member of the New York "Social Register," which lists the very rich elite from New York. Far from being rich, Tío José María was friendly with a number of ladies, most of them widowers, who found him charming and they enjoyed the stories of his life as a diplomat, his schooling at Le Rosey with his classmate who later became the Shah of Iran, his great language ability and so forth. He would regale us with many stories about these ladies and of his own life, all accompanied by not a few drinks of scotch that he happily drank. While he drank more than he should, in the month of August he never had a drink to prove to himself that he had not lost control. Being an old-fashioned gentleman, he always wore a jacket and a tie, even in the family setting.

One of Tío José María's best friends was the widow of the famed general Douglas MacArthur. And I'll tell you a story about that. After graduating from Yale Law School, while an associate at Cleary, Gottlieb, Steen & Hamilton in New York, I joined a pro-bono program sponsored by the firm that permitted associates to work full time for a few months in legal aid offices assisting the poor. I chose to work in the Bronx. One day, shortly after my return to the firm, a colleague and officemate of mine answered a call that came in. I was not in the office at the time. The lady asked for "Mr. de Lasa," and my colleague told her that I was not in and, asked her if she was one of my clients from the Bronx. The lady responded, "A client from the Bronx? Son, I am the widow of General Douglas MacArthur!" And to my consternation and regret, I learned that he answered, "Lady, if you are the widow of General MacArthur, I am Santa Claus." Well, what a mess! When I learned about the call I called Tío José María to let him know what had happened. He was totally enraged. Of course, Tío called Mrs. McArthur to explain. Weeks later, when he had calmed down, he said that Mrs. McArthur told him that she had lost his telephone number and looked him up in the telephone book where she found my name and phone number. (I am his namesake.) The firm had listed the names of all the firm's lawyers in the phone book. Things happen...

Before graduation from college, I had to decide what career to pursue. Medicine, which had been my first choice in Cuba, was not really a possibility. I was married, with three children, facing college student debts and the prospect of heavy additional debt to cover the long medical training. It was not a realistic path to follow. Also, I still harbored the hope of a return to Cuba where I think I would have followed a career in politics and government service, and I concluded medicine would not be the best choice to attain that goal. Getting a doctorate in political science became appealing and I applied to Yale and was admitted. But I was not totally convinced. It would take years to graduate and our financial situation would remain strained on what I could earn as a professor.

María Teresa and I used to go to Mass every day after her workday and on one of those days, walking in front of the law school, she asked me if I had considered the possibility of studying law. That involved only three years of studies, with financial rewards greater than being a professor. Even if I decided to become a professor, law professors have better salaries than those teaching in other disciplines. A law degree also offered many choices, like being in private practice, joining the law department of a company, clerking for judges for a time, or working at a government department or agency. The range of options was very attractive to me, and not really having a defined vocation for some other career, I decided to study law.

I had very good grades, eventually graduating *magna cum laude*, and relying on good letters of recommendations, I decided to apply to Yale and Harvard. My LSAT score was a dismal 410, placing me in the bottom 10% of the nation. When I went to see Dean Tate, the dean of admissions at Yale Law School, he told me not to worry, that my chances for admission would have been reduced if I had scored higher, but not at the top. Very high scores are the norm for admission at the top law schools, and, the dean reasoned, it would be easier to ignore my very bad score in contrast with an otherwise excellent academic record. Yale and Harvard admitted me with scholarships. While I would have preferred to go to Harvard and experience an education at another top law school located in the wonderful city of Boston, it did not make much sense to incur still more debt by leaving our house in New Haven.

I had great teachers at Yale Law School, some of whom I remember well. Guido Calabresi taught torts and each class was filled with laughter discussing the many cases we had to read. After I graduated, he became, for a few years, the dean of the law school, and was later appointed a judge to the Second Circuit Court of Appeals. This appeals court is one of the most distinguished in the country, and he now serves there as a senior judge. He lives on a farm near New Haven, where every year he would invite the students in his class for a picnic.

It was there where María Teresa and I met a few couples that, to this day, remain good friends, including, Ron and Nina Gilson, and Libby and Chris Lunding. Chris and I worked as associates at Cleary, Gottlieb, Steen and Hamilton after law school and Chris became a partner after I left the firm. We saw him and Libby often for many years after graduation. They divorced and Chris married Barbara. We have continued to enjoy a relationship with Libby, and Chris and Barbara. Our friendship with Ron and Nina is very strong. They know our children and grandchildren well and we know theirs. Ron has enjoyed a joint appointment at Stanford Law School and also at Columbia Law

School, and they divide their time between San Francisco and New York. María Teresa and Nina also see each other often when Nina is in New York.

Of the other professors who taught me at law school, Joe Goldstein, a criminal law professor, became a friend. He asked me to assist him, Alan Dershowitz and another professor in updating a widely used textbook they had written. On a number of occasions, I accompanied him to meet with Dershowitz at Harvard Law School. Dershowitz, who had been Goldstein's student at Yale Law School, joined the Harvard faculty following his graduation from Yale and became a famed criminal defense attorney. I also became close to Myers McDougal, a renowned international law scholar, and his one-time student, Michael Riesman, also on the Yale Law School faculty. All these professors whose courses I took were very friendly and I visited them quite often to discuss topics covered by their books and lectures.

McDougal and Reisman offered me in 1971 the opportunity to travel to Central America to interview political actors in El Salvador and Guatemala, do research, and write a paper on the subject of the Central American Common Market. The paper was based on an analytical political science model developed by McDougal and the political scientist Harold Laswell. For this project, I received credits equivalent to one full semester of classes and, upon graduation, I shared with another student the Ambrose Gherini Prize that carried a $500 gift. I had made a prior trip to study the Central American Common Market in the summer of my junior year in college after having obtained a school research grant. On that first trip, María Teresa and Bebé came along. On both occasions we were fortunate to have been invited to stay at the home of Fernando and Zoila Margarita García Chacón. My relationship with Fernando does indeed go back a long time.

In law school I met another president to be, Bill Clinton, and one who ran for president, but lost the election, Hillary Clinton. They were in classes following mine: Bill was class of '73, Hillary '72, and I, '71. While I met Hillary and Bill, our contacts were minimal in contrast to the interactions I had with George W. Bush next to whom I sat for one full year in our Spanish college class.

During law school, I attended a couple of meetings to discuss a possible student strike to protest the Vietnam War. A few other schools, including Harvard and Columbia, had engaged in student strikes. At one of those meetings a proposal was made to go on strike, but to request that the school allow the graduating class to take final exams. I remember my opining to the group that a strike like the one being proposed would not be effective, and described a student strike at the University of Havana that shut down the university to protest the Batista dictatorship. That was a way, I explained, that students in Cuba and in Latin America generally had historically played a non partisan and important role in influencing politics. I believe that my remarks did not really have much of an impact.

Also related to the Vietnam War was a reception held in the law school for some professors and the entering class of married students. There I met an Army lieutenant who had just returned wounded from Vietnam and had been admitted to the law school. At that moment huge protests were going on around the country to protest the U.S. military intervention in Vietnam. A typical expression of protest was the burning of U.S. flags during marches. One had recently taken place in New York where flags were burned. I told the lieutenant that I thought the burning of flags was shameful while U.S. forces were fighting a war. In a tone of voice and facial expression that conveyed understanding for my feelings, he simply responded, "It is for defending the right of the people to express their views that I went to fight in Vietnam." I felt diminished, but impacted by the lesson he had given me, of which I am mindful to this day.

While still undecided on a teaching career, I began to interview for a summer associate position in a New York law firm after my second year of law school. Many law firms conduct interviews in law schools and I interviewed with a few. Some offered me a job and others did not. I was hired by Cleary, Gottlieb, Steen & Hamilton, a prominent law firm with headquarters in New York and offices at that time in Paris, Brussels, Hong Kong, and Tokyo. The majority of summer associates are usually made offers to become regular associates after graduation. I knew of Cleary's reputation and I was interested in the firm's international practice. Jimmy Johnson, a senior partner and graduate from Yale Law School, conducted my interview. He told me of the work that the firm had done to protect the "Cuban Sugar Quota," under which Cuba guaranteed to the U.S. a preferential supply of a large amount of sugar at a price substantially higher than the world sugar price. The firm had a strong relation with Arturo Maña, a renowned Cuban lawyer, known by my family. Maña would hire Cleary as legal counsel to represent Cuba in the negotiations with the U.S. and he would spend months in Washington at the Cleary office there. Jimmy Johnson was the firm's principal contact with Maña and it was a nice coincidence that he was the partner who interviewed me. Jimmy ended up being a sponsor of mine at the firm, a neighbor in Larchmont, a tennis partner, and a good friend. And we often commuted together on the Lexington Avenue subway, which did not have air conditioning back then, and in the summer I became soaked in perspiration. Jimmy would just tell me, "José, that's character building."

My weekly salary as a summer associate was $300, the then going rate at large New York firms. That year, 1970, Cleary's rate was originally $250 and I happily accepted. Then, I learned that another prestigious law firm in New York, Cravath, Swaine & Moore, had raised the summer associate weekly salary to $300, so I called the partner who made me the offer to inform him. In a couple of hours he called me back to tell me that the weekly salary would be $300. To this day, law firms try to offer salaries competitive with those of comparable firms, and the associates learn what other firms are paying as rates go up. I ended up being called "the Spanish shop steward," a union member who represents fellow workers in negotiations with management. Of course, law firms are not unionized, and associates typically do not really negotiate. Neither did I.

During those summer weeks I spent in New York, I lived with Tío José María, sleeping on a sofa, after having a couple of drinks with him and dining more often than not on delicious beef ribs, potatoes, and salad while enjoying his stories. Many nights I wasn't able to join him for a pleasant dinner, having had to stay at the firm working. One day, I received a call from María Teresa who was pregnant telling me that she had begun to have contractions. I hurried to Grand Central Station and took the next train to New Haven, arriving on time to welcome Andrés, the next baby.

I graduated from Yale Law School in 1971 and by then I had accepted an offer from Cleary to become an associate. María Teresa and I started looking for an apartment to rent in the New York area. We soon realized we did not have enough money to live in the city and we found a small but nice apartment in Scarsdale, New York, a near suburb. The starting salary was $15,000, which was barely enough to cover the living expenses of a family with three children. It took a couple of years of saving to afford a color TV. When I worked at night at the office, which was often, I was entitled to have dinner and charge it to the firm. From time to time, I would buy the dinner at Grand Central Station and take it home to share it with María Teresa. She had a challenging, not to say hard, life raising three small children in a small apartment with a husband who several days a week would arrive home between 9 and 10 p.m. It was painful to get an occasional telephone call from her crying because of all the pressure she was under. But her resilience allowed her to carry on successfully despite the difficulties and lead a happy home.

At Cleary, in contrast with other firms, associates were not required to choose a practice specialty upon entering the firm. We could, at least for a couple of years, select areas of interest in which to work, and with the passage of time, associates would concentrate on one or two areas of practice. I chose to work in litigation and corporate financial work, both domestic and international, which involved some travel to Mexico, Central America and Brazil.

The firm also offered associates the opportunity to do *pro bono* work. I much enjoyed representing low-income clients in the Bronx. Most of my cases involved representing mothers whose children had been removed from their homes by the Bureau of Child Welfare under allegations that they had been neglected. Happily, I never had to deal with abuse cases. In the negligence cases I handled, I opposed the Bureau of Child Welfare. The contrast between the family court in the Bronx and the courts in Manhattan was pitiful. The family court where I practiced had uninformed wardens with clubs under their arms, acting as guards. And judges were occasionally very flexible in applying the law. In the first case I handled, I moved for dismissal because my client, the mother, had not been properly served according to law and as required by our Constitution. The judge, somewhat perplexed by my argument, smiled and said that the Constitution didn't really have a role in the sort of cases handled in his family court. After four months working in the Bronx, the normal period that the firm permitted the associates to volunteer *pro bono* and still receive a full salary, I returned to the firm.

I worked at Cleary during four happy years where I learned some key lessons that ranged from making sure that there were no typographical errors in any letter sent to a client, to thoroughly researching the issue at hand while keeping my seniors informed about each step in my research and reasoning. Some lawyers in other firms often sign letters to clients under the *caveat* "dictated but not read." Cleary would regard that as a mortal sin. My Cleary career began with an embarrassment. I did not pass the bar exam! Having graduated from a top law school I erroneously, not to say stupidly, failed to take the bar exam training courses. I did not make the same mistake again. I took the training courses, studied like crazy, and passed the exam I took again after a few months, during which time I felt I was under a cloud, even though the firm went out of its way not to make me feel that way.

I made many friends at Cleary. Some of them, Roger Thomas, Jim Munsell, and Jim Beery, all known to many of you, are to this day among my best friends. María Teresa and I have become particularly close to Roger and his wife Sava who we met while I was a summer associate. Sava, a Chilean lawyer, who Roger met while working on a tax research project in Chile, became a good friend of María Teresa, who is the godmother of Phillip, their youngest son. Jim Munsell and his then wife Judith, who sadly passed away some years ago, and Jim Beery and his wife Candy also became very good friends. We used to get together often for dinner at their apartments in the City. I remember well the dinner we all had at Jim and Candy's apartment the night that the early edition of the *New York Times* was to list those who had passed the second bar exam I had taken. After dinner, we all went to the corner to pick up the paper and began celebrating big time when we saw my name on the list. Jim Munsell remarried after Judith's death and we often get together with him and his wife, Vicky,

My aspiration at Cleary was to become a partner of the firm, a decision made by the partners after an associate worked for a period of more or less seven years. During my fourth year at the firm, a senior associate with whom I was working was denied partnership. He started looking for another job and interviewed for the position of Chief Legal Counsel in the Latin American operations of Bristol-Myers Squibb Company, a large healthcare company based in New York. He was offered the position, but decided to move and find a job in another city. He approached me and told me about the position with Bristol-Myers, the people he had met, the salary he was offered, and strongly suggested that I seek an interview with the company, at least to get an idea of the sort of market available to me were I to decide to seek another job. Although at that time I felt that a career in law could best be pursued practicing with a top law firm in New York, I decided to apply for the job at Bristol-Myers.

The General Counsel, the International Counsel, to whom I would report, the head of the company's International Division, and the head of the Latin American Division, who would be my client, all interviewed me. I was very impressed by both the lawyers and the business leaders I met. In a few days I was made an offer with a salary higher than my then current salary at Cleary. Before responding, I decided to speak with Jimmy Johnson and with Roger Thomas, who had recently been made a partner, and probe them on my chances of becoming a partner, a decision still three years away. Of course, neither could, or should, have made a prediction on my chances. But Roger helped me make up my mind by saying that knowing me he thought that I would probably be happier in joining the company – which turned out to be a prophetic advice. My reviews had been very good year after year, but one Cleary partner had recently told me that if a vote were then held, he would not vote in favor, and while I still had some years ahead of me to overcome his reservations, his opinion did influence my decision.

The combination of the uncertainty about becoming a partner, a decision still three years away, my sadness not to be at home as often as I wanted to have dinner with my family, and the very favorable impression I had of those I met at Bristol-Myers, along with the range of responsibilities I would have leading the Latin America legal practice and being a key leader of the Latin American business team, led to me to decide to accept the Bristol-Myers offer. That was a decision I was never to regret and my happiness with it was confirmed when, after my first day of work, Jose and Andrés met me in the early evening at the train station in Larchmont on their bicycles.

We lived in the Scarsdale apartment from 1971 to 1973 before we moved to Larchmont. Rosario Delgado, a long time friend of María Teresa, advised us that a house next to theirs on Howard Street in Larchmont had been on the market for a long time and that the owners might consider a rental. We met with the owners and told them that we were interested in buying the house, but as we did not yet have the financial means, we would need to rent for a couple of years. The deal was reached. My salary at the time increased nicely every year, so after a few months of renting we concluded that we could afford mortgage payments.

The challenge was how to raise the down payment. Mamá was the first and most important resource. She obtained a second mortgage on the house in New Haven and loaned us money. I called my good friend, Fernando, and asked him for a loan, which he immediately extended. With the down payment in hand, we signed a contract and bought the house at 5 Howard Street in Larchmont. And we were so happy! I was able to pay off the loans to Mamá and Fernando a few years later when Bristol-Myers transferred me to Brussels and my financial situation began to improve significantly.

My professional and personal life changed in very posi-
tive ways when I joined Bristol-Myers. I only had one boss, Rod
Hamel, during the 18 years that I worked there. He was what
under normal circumstances a good manager should be. He
knew how to delegate and not micromanage; how to promote
teamwork rather than having us work in silos; how to promote
high ethical standards rather than overlook them to achieve a
business objective; how to provide performance feedback on a
current basis rather than only on an annual review; and he always encouraged us to keep our focus on what the client wanted to achieve.

On my first day at work he told me that in giving my
opinion on whether this or the other action could be taken, I
should consider not only the legal consequences, but also the
public reaction to it and larger implications to the company. I
made many friends in the legal division whom I came to respect
for their legal talent and ability to deal with clients. I was fully
integrated into the senior management team of the Latin
American Division, and was thereby able to learn the business
plans before they were implemented and contribute my com-
ments on any potential legal implications. I traveled extensively
to Puerto Rico, Venezuela, Brazil, Chile, Argentina and Mexico,
where I worked closely with the business managers on a wide
range of issues having legal implications such as litigations, con-
tracts, labor matters, manufacturing, quality control, and en-
forcement of company policies. After four years as Chief Legal
Counsel for Latin America, I was transferred to Brussels as Chief

Legal Counsel for the Europe, Middle East and Africa Division ("EMEA").

Rod Hamel told me in advance of the possibility of my being transferred to Europe and suggested I begin learning French. I jumped on it, taking classes at Berlitz, a well-known language center, which provided intensive courses. I began speaking French with my mother and Tío José María, both fluent French speakers. Of course, at the beginning, I could only mutter a few words. But, little by little I improved, and after a few months I was able to have a conversation in French during which my conversation partners would correct my errors. When appointed, María Teresa and I went to Rome, then the EMEA headquarters, to start looking for a place to live, check on possible schools for the children, and for me to meet with the senior managers of the divisions and our outside counsel.

We were thrilled with the prospect of moving to Rome, the Eternal City, where María Teresa had been born and lived for three years, two of which in the Vatican, where her family had to move during World War II. Her father was the Cuban representative to the Vatican, and when the War broke out, they had to leave Rome, along with other diplomats from countries in the Allied forces who were at war with Italy. The Pope invited them to the Vatican, a sovereign city-state, where they were provided with apartments in which to live. Our enthusiasm with the possibility of living in Rome was short-lived. At that time, Italy was trying to contain the Red Brigades, a left wing paramilitary organization, responsible for many violent incidents, including assassinations and kidnappings. After the kidnapping and assassination of Aldo Moro, a prominent politician who had been Prime Minister of Italy, the company concluded that Rome was no longer a suitable place for its EMEA headquarters and decided to move it to Brussels in Belgium.

A few months before our move to Brussels in 1978, Jose injured his knee while playing soccer in Larchmont. He developed a fungal infection that required an operation. It was not fully cured until months later, following another operation in Brussels, and a two-month hospitalization taking a newly discovered antifungal medication. He was in a wheelchair when we moved to Brussels. Carlos had been born in March of that year. It was a challenge to move to another country and set up a home with four children, one of them temporarily crippled, and a four-month-old baby. Elena came to our rescue. She took a leave of absence from her teaching position in a New Haven public school and went to live with us in Brussels. What a blessing that was! Her help began immediately by taking Jose and Carlos to fly with her to Brussels two or three weeks after we had flown there; had the chance to wait for our furniture to arrive; and began settling into the new house.

Our stay in Brussels was a highlight in our lives from every point of view. Our house was in Waterloo, a Brussels suburb, and Bebé, Jose and Andrés went to a nearby English speaking school where they began learning French. Our life as a family was strengthened as María Teresa and I had closer contact with the children who, in Larchmont, were accustomed to engage in separate activities, often sleeping at friends' houses, and not fully engaged among themselves and with us. I well remember our first Christmas, going on a short ride to another country to buy our Christmas tree. We went to Aachen in Germany, visited the city, including its beautiful cathedral where Charlemagne is buried, saw the people excitedly doing their Christmas shopping, and bought the Christmas tree. Mission accomplished.

There were so many trips to so many countries during our time in Brussels! One that I particularly remember, and still laugh about, took place shortly after our arrival in Brussels. We went to Amsterdam in Holland for a short visit, just to go to another country. Shortly after I parked our car, a Citroen family car with three rows of seats, the children started giggling and María Teresa, with a reproachful look on her face, said to me, "look where you have parked!" I had not noticed that the street had a row of little houses, one next to the other, with large windows behind which sat semi-nude ladies engaged in the world's oldest profession. Some of the curtains were drawn because the lady was occupied or simply not at work. I don't remember how we explained this to the children, or whether we even offered an explanation. I quickly moved the car and found a more suitable parking space.

We vacationed as a family in Italy, Greece, Spain, and in shorter trips to London. Mamá, who had lived in Europe and Tío José María, who had studied and lived there, had been telling us about the wonders of Europe, and we were able to experience it. Each country was very different from the other, with very different customs, people, and languages, yet with a common denominator of beauty, exuberant enjoyment of life, and shared history.

My professional life was challenging and enjoyable. First, I had to establish my credentials, being a young lawyer and having never been in Europe before. I had to learn how to work with business clients and outside counsel, senior in age to me, and accustomed to working very independently. I supervised three lawyers: Ross Foertmeyer, Alastair Jackson and Cormac O'Malley. I had a particularly strong relationship with Alastair, a British lawyer living in London, who I saw often in Brussels and occasionally in London as well. My principal client was André Thierry, a Frenchman who was the head of the EMEA division. While he had an apartment in Brussels and spent most of his time in the Brussels headquarters office, he held many meetings in Paris where he had lived all his life. He sort of adopted me, like the son he never had. We constantly traveled together and while in Brussels often dined together. He taught me how to enjoy some new dishes and foods I had never tried, while having a nice bottle of wine.

At first, I would introduce various business topics into our conversation, but early on he stopped me from doing that saying, "José, a meal is like a ceremony to be enjoyed as such and business topics are not really suitable to be discussed." Jean Blondlet, another senior EMEA manager, resided in Brussels and became a very good friend. He and his wife often invited us to her country home in the Ardennes to spend Saturdays or Sundays relaxing, with wonderful meals, and traveling around to visit places in the heavily forested Ardennes region. One day we spent the day visiting the museums and war memorials where the Battle of the Bulge, the last German offensive in the Western Front, took place. The Germans attacked the U.S. forces with over 400,000 men and 1,000 tanks. The U.S. forces won the battle after many days of fighting. It is regarded as the longest and bloodiest battle fought by the U.S. in World War II, with heavy casualties on both sides of over two hundred thousand men. It was moving to have visited the scene of the battle and the memorial.

After three wonderful years in Brussels we returned to New York in August 1981 sailing from Southampton on the Queen Elizabeth II (or QE2), a large and famous trans-Atlantic ship of the British Cunard line. I was looking forward, crazy of me some of you might think, to encountering some rough weather with big waves, which would remind me of crossing many years earlier the Mona Passage in 10 to 15 foot waves in a 28-foot Bertram. I was disappointed that the 963 ft. QE2 only encountered very calm seas.

We returned to our Larchmont home, which we had rented during our stay in Brussels, and promptly sold it, moving to a large house also in Larchmont at 88 Park Avenue in December of that year. We would have enjoyed staying in Europe another couple of years, but we were very happy to return and be close to our family and friends. Mamá, Naty and Elena visited us often. We became members of the Larchmont Yacht Club, which we still enjoy, although we no longer live in Larchmont. We renewed our contacts with many friends, including those in Larchmont whom we had met through Rosario and Manuel Delgado. We also started going to Puerto Rico to spend time with María Teresa's parents and brothers.

I joined the parish council at Saint Augustine Church and renewed our friendship with Father Benedict Groeschel, who lived at Trinity House, just a few blocks from us. Fr. Groeschel had just founded The Franciscan Friars of the Renewal, a Franciscan Capuchin Order, working principally with the poor in houses of the Order in Harlem and the Bronx where I occasionally visited to volunteer. Jose and Andrés would also accompany me from time to time on Saturday visits to work in a soup kitchen in the Bronx handled by the Missionaries of Charity, founded by Mother Teresa of Calcutta, now a Saint. We joined a group of friends to form a prayer group that met every two weeks for dinner, to pray the rosary, and to have a discussion on one or more Bible passages. The friends were, Rosario and Manuel, Raquel and Mario Suárez, Olga and Pablo Torres, and Luis and Jacqueline Parajón, all long time members of the *Agrupación Católica Universitaria*.

My new position as International Counsel for Bristol-Myers required my traveling worldwide. My first trip in the fall of 1981 was to Asia, an area I had never visited. It was a three-week trip so I decided to spend a few days on vacation with

María Teresa before departing. A colleague of mine suggested Block Island as a destination, saying that it would remind us of Europe, with the hills, stonewalls, farms and ocean cliffs, all of remarkable beauty. Rosario and Manuel joined us for a three-day weekend visit and the four of us became captivated by the Island, where we now own a house, and where for over 30 years we spent two-week family vacations renting a home in the summers.

Mamá and Elena would join us for a few days on our vacations, and Naty's girls and spouses have also rented houses there over many years. Our children and grandchildren much enjoy Block Island. It was there where Caroline and Jose married, and where Bebé and Richard, and Caroline Claire and Carlos became engaged, and where Kyle and Andrés owned a house for a few years. And it was there where, especially after building our own house, we made some good friends, notably Jack and Helen Lynch. I became Jack's partner in sharing the maintenance expenses of his boat, "Go-Fish," on which we enjoy many fishing outings, often accompanied by friends and some of my children and grandchildren. Jim Beery and his son-in-law, Andy Miller, don't miss an opportunity to join us while spending their summer vacations on Block Island. Of course, Sam, Jim's grandson, who brings us much luck in catching fish, always comes along. Block Island became, and likely will remain, an important destination for the extended family and us. María Teresa and I recently purchased a plot in the Block Island Cemetery for our ashes to be buried there.

Bristol-Myers and Squibb were merged in 1989 and I was appointed Chief Legal Counsel of the worldwide pharmaceutical and nutritional business that were to be managed from the Squibb headquarters in Princeton, New Jersey. I had offices both in New York and Princeton and I generally would spend Monday through Thursday in Princeton and Friday in New York. The job was a challenge, since I had to integrate into my legal department the Squibb legal staff and earn their respect and recognition as their leader. I kept traveling on company business, although not as often as before. In 1993, I was appointed Secretary of the company and returned to the New York office full time. I was then at a very senior level, continuing to report to Rod Hamel who was the General Counsel, and now having as clients the Chief Executive Officer (CEO) and the board of directors.

For a number of years, Rod and other senior managers had considered me as the most likely candidate to become General Counsel upon Rod's expected retirement in early 1995. I also fully shared that expectation and it was a big disappointment for me to learn that it was an aspiration unlikely to be realized. At the time, the company was engaged in two large and very threatening litigations and the CEO decided to pass me over and appoint as General Counsel the attorney from a law firm handling one of the litigations. When it became evident to me that I would not get the job, I started looking for a general counsel position in another company. I knew that the Abbott Laboratories General Counsel, whom I knew well, had recently resigned. I called him and he put me in touch with Abbott's head of Human Resources. My first interview was with a headhunter from the search firm being used by Abbott and shortly thereafter I was invited to visit Abbott in Chicago, where I met with Duane Burnham, the CEO, and Thomas Hodgson, the President of Abbott. The following week both María Teresa and I were invited to Chicago to have dinner with Burnham, Hodgson and their spouses. Obviously, the objective of the dinner was to meet María Teresa. We returned that night to White Plains on a company plane, and the next day I received a call from the head of Human Resources making me an offer.

The compensation, benefits, position title and other benefits that were offered were great, but something important was missing from the package. If I accepted the Abbott offer, I would have to retire from Bristol-Myers at age 53, two years short of the earliest retirement age of 55, at which time I would be entitled to enjoy a nice pension. I had told the head of Human Resources at Abbott on more than one occasion that if an offer was to be made it needed to be subject to a contract under which I would be paid out an amount equivalent to the then present value of my Bristol-Myers pension in the event that Abbott were to terminate my employment. I felt I could not take the risk of foregoing a nice Bristol-Myers pension in that event and I therefore declined the Abbott offer. Two months or so thereafter, I received a call from Duane Burnham telling me that the company had been reviewing other possible candidates for the position, but that they liked me, "as well as your lovely wife," and that the contract I wanted would be part of the deal. I accepted the offer and joined the company in December 1994.

María Teresa was sad to leave Larchmont and the children and move to Chicago, a city unknown to her. She asked me not to sell the Larchmont house so we could have it available in the summer and gather the family during Christmas and Easter holidays. We indeed spent those holidays in Larchmont and she spent the summers there. I flew to Larchmont every weekend in the summer. It was a wise decision on María Teresa's part, which helped lessen the impact of family separation and which made sense financially, since the value of the Larchmont house continued to increase over the years more than offsetting the cost of maintaining it during that time.

Bebé had married Richard in 1989 and was living in Boston. Andrés married Kyle in 1997, and Jose married Caroline in 2000, and both boys remained living in the house until their marriages. After we moved to Chicago, Carlos first went to Portsmouth Abbey School in New Hampshire for one year, then moved to Chicago to live with us and to go to school there, and finally returned to Larchmont in 1996, finishing High School in Mamaroneck, New York, while living at the Larchmont house.

We enjoyed our Chicago apartment in a corner building on Lake Shore Drive and Elm Street, which was very close to the Magnificent Mile, and right across from North Beach. The sunrise view of Lake Michigan from our living room was beautiful. We began enjoying urban life in the beautiful city of Chicago and María Teresa became engaged in a number of activities, particularly the International Women's Association, a group of women with significant international connections including women expatriates. I joined the board of directors of the Chicago Council on Global Affairs, which held frequent meetings on important global issues and occasionally engaged world leaders as speakers. The Chicago Council launched a task force to study the impact of immigrants who had entered the U.S., mostly undocumented. The task force, of which I was a member, was composed of some 20 representatives from a variety of entities, small and large, including businesses, labor unions, universities, research centers, and government. After three months studying the matter, backed mostly by statistical information, the task force submitted a report that received a lot of attention, especially in Washington. Its principal conclusion was that immigrants, most of whom were undocumented, were as workers, consumers and taxpayers, a significant asset to the economic life of the country. I wish that the contributions that immigrants to our country make were better known and recognized. Maybe one day the powers that be in Washington will finally pass the necessary laws and regulations to deal with this complicated issue that our country faces. In addition to the Chicago Council on Global Affairs, I also served on the board of directors of the Chicago Children's Museum during my time in Chicago.

We made some very good friends in Chicago, notably Enrique and Irene Sosa, Cuban Americans, whom we knew before, but our real friendship began while we were in Chicago. After his retirement from Dow Chemical, Enrique moved to Chicago to join Amoco, a large oil company headquartered there, as the president of its chemical division. Our friendship was then and remains today most enjoyable. They live now in Key Biscayne and we see them often while we are there in the winter months. On a number of occasions we have been invited with other friends of theirs for one-week trips to the Bahamas in their beautiful yacht. Enrique and I both serve on the executive committee of the Cuba Study Group, which affords us another opportunity to see each other. We also became good friends with Stephen and Laura Gates. Steve, who sadly passed away recently, was the General Counsel of Amoco and Laura was Vice President for Museum Affairs of The Field Museum of Natural History. We met them shortly after our arrival in Chicago in a corporate box at a Chicago Bulls game, watching Michael Jordan in one of his many stellar performances. It was at that game that I learned that Steve and I had been classmates at Yale, graduating in the Class of 1968. Our friendship continued through years after we all left Chicago.

A key factor in making our 10-plus years in Chicago very enjoyable was that my niece, Natalia Delgado, was living in Chicago when we arrived. She was married then to Rodrigo del Canto, and had two small daughters, Catalina and Isabel. We lived with them for a few days when we first arrived. We saw each other frequently and shared dinners at least once a week. In the summertime, when María Teresa was in Larchmont, I had dinner at their house, or at Natalia's apartment following their divorce, almost daily, thus helping me cope with María Teresa's absence. Natalia graduated from the University of Michigan Law School and was a partner at Jenner & Block, a prominent Chicago law firm, and a few years after I arrived in Chicago, she moved to the law firm of Goldberg Kohn, also as a partner. We often talked about legal issues, law firms, and generally the practice of law. When she divorced Rodrigo, she moved to an apartment located almost next door to ours.

Merritt Fox, my classmate from Yale College and Yale Law School and a good friend ever since, who had been divorced for some time visited with us a couple of times in Chicago. On one of those occasions, while he was visiting with his son, Edward, we invited Natalia to join us for dinner at a restaurant. Natalia had previously met Merritt when he first joined the faculty at the University of Michigan Law School and they had seen each other once a year when she attended the annual Committee of Visitors of the Law School on which she served for over 10 years. When we watched Natalia and Merritt looking and smiling at each other that night at the dinner in Chicago, María Teresa and I became convinced that an attraction to each other had commenced. They married in Chicago a few years later.

Another person whose friendship and help also contributed to our enjoyable Chicago experience was Ana María Vásquez, who became a warm and always smiling friend, and who many in my extended family, including Natalia, already knew.

Ana María had lived in Chicago for many years, and had many friends, as well as a large network of connections in business and civic circles. She was always ready to help us during our years in Chicago. Finally, I should mention a few classmates of mine from Colegio de Belén in Havana who were then living in Chicago and with whom we met from time to time with our spouses: Antonio Navarrete, Oswaldo López, Alfredo González and Fernando Casado. Needless to say, during our years in Chicago, we had many family and friends visiting us, including our good friends, José and Gloria Rionda.

I had a terrific experience working at Abbott. My first task was to try to become accepted and recognized by the 100-plus lawyers in the legal division as their leader. It was a task no different from the one I faced in dealing with the Squibb lawyers after the merger with Bristol-Myers, except that at Abbott it was more difficult. At the beginning of my tenure, all the lawyers were from the Midwest, and I being from New York, with a Spanish accent, made me appear to them as a "foreigner." Moreover, two lawyers in the Law Department had aspired to be appointed general counsel and had made that wish known to senior management, so for some lawyers in the department my having been selected as General Counsel was a disappointment. I also had to learn about the major legal issues facing the company and the prevailing thoughts of the lawyers in the legal department and of the managers who were our clients. I immediately began to hold one-on-one meetings with the senior lawyers in the department and all the lawyers who reported directly to them. I presented myself to them as their eager leader that needed their help. I asked each of them: "put yourself in my place as General Counsel and let me know what changes you would make in the department to make it better." Their feedback was an enormous source of information for me and, perhaps more importantly, it helped me build trust with them for not appearing to be arrogant or indifferent to their views. The interviews were a big hit with the department lawyers.

The second task I initially undertook at Abbott was to interview the senior managers and some of their direct reports, asking for their views on the performance of the legal department, their assessment of the lawyers with whom they worked, the changes they thought I should make, and their requirements or expectations for the legal function. Armed with all this feedback, I proceeded to make a few personnel changes, including asking a couple of lawyers to look for a new job, and reorganized my senior legal staff.

I developed a good relationship with Duane Burnham, the CEO, whom I promptly asked what he expected of me, how frequently we should have interactions, and what form of communication he preferred. As General Counsel, I had to exercise independent judgment while being supportive. If I had to say "no" to some action being proposed, I would first offer other appropriate options to accomplish the same goal for management's consideration. Fortunately, I never had to go above the CEO to the board of directors and challenge his opinion or action, a move that I would have been obligated to make, if a possible violation of law was at stake. I was also the Chief Compliance Officer of the company, which added an important dimension to my responsibilities.

As General Counsel, I made the final decision on selecting outside counsel. A few law firms, with which the company had a long-standing relationship, handled the vast majority of matters that needed to be referred to outside counsel. It was only on a few major matters, typically including litigation or acquisitions that I intervened to ratify the selection made by my direct reports or to propose the selection of another law firm. The quality of the firm was always the key factor in the selection, but the control of legal fees became an important factor as well, and we were able in most cases to negotiate the fees in advance. I was a member of the Association of General Counsel, an organization comprising the general counsels of the largest 80 or 90 companies in the U.S. and a sprinkling of large foreign companies. The Association met twice per year, and the subject of how to control legal fees was discussed every year.

During my time at Abbott, I lived in Chicago whereas Abbott is headquartered in a suburb, very close to beautiful Lake Forest, Illinois an hour drive away. Each morning on my way to work, I began my driving at 6 a.m. listening to the news and on the return trip listening to tapes of Father Benedict Groeschel. On my way in, I stopped at a church in Lake Forest to hear Mass and arrived at work shortly before 8 a.m. I began my ride home after work at around 6 p.m. when the traffic was heavier and normally it would take me about 90 minutes to get to Chicago. Listening to the news, tapes of Father Groeschel, and taking occasional business calls, made the ride not too burdensome. My doctor, dentist, and barber were all located in Lake Forest. I went to the gym at the Abbott facilities several times a week and typically ate lunch in my office or in the company cafeteria. On average, once a week I would travel to Chicago to have lunch with Abbott outside lawyers or to attend meetings of organizations to which I belonged. Happily, for those trips a company car with a chauffeur was made available to me so I would conduct a good amount of business on the phone and catch up on reading in the two hours I spent in the car.

The weekends were most enjoyable. Maria Teresa and I would spend hours taking walks around the city, especially along the gorgeous shoreline, and in its beautiful parks. Since the 1830s, the official motto of Chicago has been "City in a Garden." Among its gardens and parks, Millennium Park became an instant hit after it was completed in 2004 and is the top attraction in the Midwest, and one of the 10 most-visited tourist sites in the country. María Teresa and I both began playing golf, however poorly, and joined a nice golf club where we used to play nine holes during the season. (Countless hours of golf lessons have yet to make my score break 100.) I also joined a hunting lodge near Chicago and during the hunting season would go there almost every weekend to shoot pheasants. Miles White, the Abbott CEO, (more about him later), and Marc

Whitehead, a lawyer whom I had met, were my usual companions on the shoots. Marc, and his wife Tracy, became good friends.

I met William Daley, then a senior partner at the law firm of Mayer Brown & Platt, one of Abbott's principal outside counsel, who had renegotiated the Panamá Canal treaty and for a while served as Chief of Staff in the Barack Obama White House. At the time, we were trying to place Carlos in Loyola High School. Bob Hellman, the chairman of Mayer Brown, who became a good friend, told me not to worry, for he knew how to get Carlos into that school. Bob introduced me to his partner Bill Daley, alumnus of St Ignatius, another Jesuit school in Chicago, whose brother was Richard Daley, the popular Chicago mayor, and Bill Daley's intervention facilitated Carlos' admission. Carlos had many difficulties with his studies in previous schools due to an ADD (attention deficit disorder) condition and also because he was suffering from a circadian sleep disorder, which kept him awake for hours at night and made him sleepy in the morning. Through some friends of his, and through his brother Jose, Carlos determined that he had those conditions (which were later medically confirmed). Following treatment, he graduated from high school back in Larchmont and enrolled in the SUNY Maritime School in New York graduating in due course. He has since followed a very successful career in the Merchant Marine business.

The Abbott board meetings, four or five per year, were preceded by a dinner of the directors and the most senior managers. At one of those meetings, one of the directors, who knew I liked to hunt, asked me if I had read a recent article in Forbes Magazine featuring Los Ombues, a renowned shooting lodge in Argentina. I had read it, as had this director. In a minute, two or three directors, also fond of the shooting sport, intervened in the conversation and ended up asking me to try to organize a trip to Los Ombues. Myles White, the CEO, who overheard the conversation said, "I'm going on that trip!" The meeting was held on a Friday, as was customary, and the very next day I was teaching Miles how to shoot in the clay-shooting club to which I belonged. Miles is a natural shot and hunting has become a passion for him.

Over the years a group of directors and some senior managers including myself traveled to Los Ombues (to hunt for duck, mourning doves and partridge) as well as to shooting lodges in Spain for the red-legged partridge, and the UK and Czech Republic for pheasants. Some of our wives, including María Teresa, came along on some of those trips. On the Los Ombues trip, while we hunted, they visited the beautiful Iguazú Falls, the largest waterfall system in the world, on the border of Argentina and Brazil, before joining us at Los Ombues for the last day of the three-day shoot. From there we went to Buenos Aires for a two-day visit. These were most enjoyable trips and afforded the group an opportunity to discuss business issues in a relaxed and friendly atmosphere.

Several years after my retirement from Abbott, I returned to Los Ombues with my own guests: my sons, Andrés and Carlos, my son-in-law, Richard, my grandson and Richard's son, Edward, and my brother Miguel. A few friends also accompanied Miguel. I will never forget the joy of that trip with my sons (except for Jose who you will remember couldn't hunt because he had to face the statue of St. Francis of Assisi every morning while getting dressed in his closet), a grandson, and my brother. It was a wonderful opportunity to be with my family, engaged in an activity we all love, in a most friendly atmosphere.

In 2002, I began experiencing what I suspected were symptoms of heart disease. While running on a treadmill in the office gym, I first took notice of some numbness in the left upper arm. A few days later, while hunting with Steve Olsen, my niece Cristina's husband, at his Blooming Grove Club in Pennsylvania, I again experienced the numbness. It was on a Friday and on the next day we were having a party at the Larchmont Yacht Club to celebrate my 60th birthday anniversary. María Teresa and I did not mention my issue to family or friends. By the following Tuesday, I was seeing Dr. Eric Topol, the head of Cardiology at the Cleveland Clinic, and after an exercise stress test, which I failed, and cardiac catheterization, I was told I needed a bypass immediately, since the lateral anterior descending artery, also known as the "Widowmaker," was over 90% clogged. Early on Wednesday morning, I had bypass surgery on the Widowmaker. It was a success. While not really afraid, I felt some uneasiness given the doctor's warning that I urgently needed a bypass, because the Widowmaker was almost completely blocked. On the way to surgery, I kept re-membering St. Paul's passage in one of his letters to the Corinthians: "No eye has seen, nor ear heard, nor has it entered into the heart of man, what God has prepared for those who love him." I was comforted by the passage.

The operating room was filled with doctors and nurses engaged in a variety of activities. My brother Miguel had a bypass operation at the Cleveland Clinic a year earlier and he told me that following the operation he had great difficulty having a bowel movement, so, when the anesthesiologist asked me if I needed anything before being put to sleep, I said, "yes, please insert a suppository before taking me out of here." Everyone in the room looked at me, some perplexed and some laughing and the anesthesiologist smiling said to me, "Don't worry José." These were the last words I heard before an injection knocked me out.

Family and friends would call me to say how sorry they felt for me and my answer was that I was not sorry, but happy that God arranged to send me the numbness and I was able to have surgery before experiencing a massive heart attack. I started working on a reduced schedule some three weeks after the operation, but it took me over two months to fully recover. Mamá had a heart condition and died of a heart attack, my brother Miguel had a bypass, and my grandfather Fabián also died of a heart attack. So, children, be aware that heart disease runs in the family, and, depending on your age, start getting checked!

I spent four days in the hospital and another three days at a hotel in Cleveland. I began walking around with María Teresa to regain my strength. We then flew back to Chicago on a company plane and I began convalescing at home, but remained fully connected to the office both by the daily correspondence delivered to our apartment and frequent phone calls with my staff. That Christmas we spent in Franconia, New Hampshire, at Bebé and Richard's home. I remember how cold it was. We were in a nice room in the basement, but with poor heating. At night, I read books covered by blankets and turned pages by blowing into them instead of bringing my arm from under the blankets. During the day, we would take walks, which doctors insisted were very important in my rehabilitation. On one occasion, while walking near the house, a police car approached to tell us we should go back home because there was a Rottweiler dog on the loose, which might not be friendly. Of course, I could not walk fast, and I think my blood pressure probably rose on our way back home for some fear of running into an unfriendly Rottweiler. A couple of days after Christmas we flew to Miami, happily again on a company plane, to spend two weeks in our Buttonwood, Key Largo townhouse.

Our friends, Carlitos and Betty, had two apartments next to each other in Buttonwood and we used to rent one of them in the summer to go with the children fishing, playing tennis, water skiing, and boating in the beautiful Florida Everglades. María Teresa, Betty, Carlitos and I would often have a bottle of champagne on the boat while watching the beautiful sunsets, reminding ourselves how blessed we had been despite the fact that we had lost Cuba. Their son, Calixto, is our godson, and he and I used to go fishing together, eventually becoming partner owners of two nice boats, both named "Alegría," on which we fished in Florida and the Bahamas. When I took the Abbott job and moved to Chicago, Carlitos and Betty sold us one of the townhouses and we continued to enjoy Buttonwood for a few years until we sold the townhouse and purchased the apartment in Casa del Mar in Key Biscayne. Carlitos and Betty also sold theirs at about the same time and also bought an apartment in Casa del Mar. A couple of years later, our friends Rosario and Manuel also bought an apartment there, where they now reside. Luckily, we continue to share with these good friends many happy moments.

I told Duane Burnham, the Abbott CEO who hired me, that I would be retiring after 10 years of service. And in 2005, that is what I did. All our children and their spouses were invited to come to Chicago to attend my retirement party. They all were able to attend, except Jose and Caroline who were then living in New Zealand. My years at Abbott had been professionally very challenging, but also most enjoyable. Both, Duane Burnham and Miles White, the CEOs for whom I worked, remain good friends. Abbott provided me with the opportunity to fulfill my professional ambition and financially secure my retirement.

While we toyed with the idea of staying in Chicago, in a city and life that we had fully enjoyed, we wanted to return to

119

Larchmont and be closer to our children. Andres and Kyle had bought the Park Avenue Larchmont house from us a couple of years earlier when they returned from London, and we started looking for a new house a year or so before my retirement. In the process, Rosario, our friend and realtor, showed María Teresa a beautiful house on Pryer Lane in Larchmont and she loved it, as I did too after visiting it. We bought it, and Manuel, our friend and stellar architect, drew the architectural plan to renovate the house. We hired the contractor that Manuel recommended who did a very nice job. When we moved back from Chicago to Larchmont, the renovation had not yet been finished and Rosario and Manuel invited us to stay at their house for a couple of weeks until we could move into the house. The realtor and the architect provided a full suite of services!

When I retired from Abbott, I joined the law firm of Baker & McKenzie, one of the largest in the world, which I had used as an outside counsel while at both Bristol-Myers and Abbott. My position was "Of Counsel," which means an attorney who is employed by a law firm, not as an associate or partner, and is typically used for an attorney who is transitioning from a previous legal position. While some lawyers designated as "Of Counsel" practice law, I did not; and I worked on a part-time basis. I offered advice to members and associates of the firm, principally to inform them about client expectations of outside counsel performance. In addition, I visited with some General Counsel clients of the firm to offer advice on what, in my opinion, were the do's and don'ts of an effective General Counsel; and I also gave some corporate governance and compliance talks to groups of clients. While not my primary function, I helped to bring new clients to the firm. I organized meetings of General Counsel clients of the firm, for them to discuss among themselves issues or matters of concern, whether legal or involving the management of their department, and to share their views on how to handle them. I prepared the tentative agenda for the discussions, acted as facilitator during the meetings, and usually asked one or two partners of the firm to attend the meetings and be prepared to provide advice on legal matters that might be discussed.

During my time at Baker, I was invited by a large Chinese oil company to visit Beijing and give a conference on law department organization and corporate governance. It was my first trip to China and María Teresa joined me. Our friend, Fernando, also joined us on the trip. Before arriving in Beijing, we first visited Shanghai. We were so impressed by this modern city filled with skyscrapers with many more under construction, which was in many respects similar to any other big city in the western world. While there, we had the opportunity to travel on the Shanghai Maglev train (Magnetic Levitation), the fastest in the world, able to reach a high speed of 267 miles per hour. From Shanghai we traveled to Xian, in central China and, among other tourist attractions, visited the mausoleum of the first emperor of the Qin Dynasty, which has a tomb that had been excavated and which houses the famous Terracotta Army.

It is a large collection of terracotta sculptures depicting the army of the Qin emperor that was buried with him to protect the emperor in his afterlife. From there we went to Beijing to spend three days. I gave my conference and visited with other Chinese companies clients of the firm. We were able to visit many other interesting places including principally Tiananmen Square, one of the largest plazas in the world, containing monuments and museums and which was the site of many important events in Chinese history. They included, sadly, the military suppression of a protest in 1989 where hundreds of civilian protesters were killed by the Chinese military.

The growth of China during the last several decades has been phenomenal due to the introduction of capitalism and a substantial free enterprise system. While it continues to be a centrally planned economy, and the state controls the political system, it allows a large measure of free market activity. I spent the whole trip thinking about Cuba and being envious of the progress achieved in China. I absolutely do not aspire to have Cuba adopt a Chinese-style system, where democracy is absent and basic human rights ignored, but do wish that Cuba, in what I hope will be a process of change to restore democracy and human rights, would imitate the Chinese by drastically improving its economic system through market oriented reforms. My visits to clients of the firm, both abroad and in the U.S., continued until my retirement from Baker in 2015.

Over the last few years, a few sad family events have taken place. Carlos and Caroline-Claire's first child, Francisco, died within 24 hours after he was born, but it was a blessing that he did, for he was born with very severe physical impairments. I baptized him in the Yale New Haven Hospital with tears in my eyes, but thanking God for calling him. I now have a baby angel as a grandson. Caroline and Carlos were aware during the pregnancy that the fetus was extremely compromised and María Teresa and I recognize that their handling of Francisco's pregnancy and his death was admirable. We also suffered two other important losses: the premature death of my brother-in-law, Miguel Figueroa, and the death of my brother, Miguel. Although not in the sad category, in recent years I had to undergo three back surgeries to address spinal stenosis and a synovial cyst. In the process, my doctors fused three lumbar vertebrae resulting in my losing an appreciable amount of flexibility.

TRAVELS

My jobs have provided me an opportunity to travel around the world, more often than not accompanied by María Teresa, and some of these trips I have already mentioned. Following my retirement from Abbott we have continued traveling, and a description of some notable trips follows.

We visited India twice, in 2010 and 2012, with each trip lasting three weeks. Our travels covered many important regions and cities, including, New Delhi, Mumbai, Hyderabad, Jaipur, Agra, Varanasi, Amritsar, and Dharamshala. India is the seventh-largest country by area, inhabited by over 1.2 billion people, with many religions, principally, Hinduism, Islam and Buddhism. India has millions of Muslims, and many left the country after the Partition of India in 1947 and the creation of two independent dominions, India and Pakistan, all as part of the process of the subcontinent obtaining independence from British rule. Partition displaced 15 million people, as many Muslims moved to Pakistan and many Hindus had to resettle into India. Ever since the Partition the two countries have had a very tense relationship, involving a few wars. Despite their animosity, today these countries maintain a fairly stable diplomatic relations, marred by occasional bloody skirmishes in Kashmir, a region subject to a territorial dispute over which wars have been fought. I hope that India and Pakistan, both nuclear powers, will be able to maintain peaceful relations.

India is a captivating country, with a vast cultural diversity. It is remarkable that so many languages, religions, and races coexist in what is the most populous democracy in the world. While walking in towns we were exposed to things and activities we had never seen: Sacred cows moving around us and occasionally entering the shops we were visiting, and cow dung scattered on the street, making it a challenge to avoid while walking. In the space of one block, we saw by the side of the street a dentist, shoe repairman, and florist all at work, and a man urinating against a wall in a corner, with many people hurriedly walking around. I remember a different scene in Mumbai walking early in the morning to go to Mass at a nearby Catholic church, which are common in that part of India where many Christians live, and seeing a family that had been sleeping on a sidewalk waking up and together swiftly preparing to begin a new day.

In Varanasi, a city in northern India regarded as the Hindu spiritual capital, we walked by the shore of the Ganges River deemed to have sacred waters and where funeral rites are performed. It was stirring to watch some burning pyres where bodies were being cremated and the ashes then laid in the river, all in the belief of achieving reincarnation or a new life. It was also specially significant for us to have visited the museum dedicated to Mahatma Ghandi in New Delhi where this leader of the India independence movement against British rule lived the last months of his life and where he was assassinated in 1948. His nonviolent civil disobedience led to the country's independence and inspired many civil right movements around the world. In these two trips we visited amazing places, one of which was the Taj Mahal, a beautiful ivory-white mausoleum built over 400 years ago by a Mughal emperor in memory of his favorite wife and considered a jewel of Muslim art and a world-famous architectural beauty.

A free enterprise system in India has over the years generated significant economic growth with micro-enterprise playing an important role. During a bus ride traveling I don't remember where, we visited a tiny sugar mill set just a few yards off the road. It was operating with some eight workers and producing raw sugar in a space not bigger than a basketball court. Truly impressive! I suggest that as you make travel plans, put India as one of the top destinations on your list. I do not recommend that you travel cheaply in India, unless you happen to be a truly adventurous traveler. One way or the other you'll never forget the trip you make to India.

A highlight in our second trip to India was our meeting with the Dalai Lama, the spiritual leader of the Tibetan people and the most revered Buddhist figure in the world. The meeting was arranged by a second cousin of mine, María Luisa Broch, known in the family as "Tica" and of whom we are very fond. Tica had worked as an interpreter for the United Nations for close to 40 years. During that time, she became a Buddhist and a good friend of the Dalai Lama, serving as his interpreter during 10 of those years while he traveled around Europe. When Tica retired from the U.N., she moved to Dharamshala, a hillside city on the edge of the Himalayas, where the Dalai Lama sought refuge after the persecution of Tibetan Buddhists by China. When Tica learned that we were making a second trip to India, she offered to arrange the meeting. Accompanied by our close friends Roger and Sava Thomas, we spent three days in Dharamshala, visiting some Buddhist temples, and staying at Kashmir Cottage, the house of Ringari Rinpoche, the younger brother of the Dalai Lama and a good friend of Tica. We had the pleasure of meeting him and his wife who, interestingly, while being Buddhists, had attended Jesuit schools in India – a tribute to the value of a Jesuit education.

The meeting with the Dalai Lama took place at his residence and we, the Thomases and Tica spent close to one hour speaking with him. It was very moving. This saintly person is a warm, smiling and charismatic human being. He mentioned briefly his visits with popes and world leaders, including U.S. presidents. And in reference to the principal tenets of Buddhism we talked about the similarities Buddhism has with Christianity. He asked about the situation in Cuba and I told him that Raúl Castro was in the process of making some economic changes, but that the country continued to follow a failed communist model. I told him that a favorite prayer for us Cuban-Americans was to ask God, "to call Fidel Castro (still alive at the time) and to welcome him with the same enthusiasm with which we send Fidel to Him." The Dalai Lama couldn't stop laughing, and Tica told us that afterwards, when traveling with him, she has heard him repeat the joke.

Our travels abroad included a seven-day walk of 80 miles in October 2013, from the town of Sarría to Santiago de Compostela in Spain, in a pilgrimage sponsored by Saint Ignatius Church, our parish in New York. The "Camino de Santiago," in English known as "St. James's Way," is the pilgrimage route to the Shrine of the Apostle Saint James the Great in the Cathedral of Santiago de Compostela in the province of Galicia. The pilgrimage to this shrine became the most renowned of medieval pilgrimages. Hundreds of thousands (in 2014 over 200,000) pilgrims set out from points across Europe to make their way to Santiago, most of them by foot, some by bicycle, and some even on horses or donkeys, most staying in pilgrims hostels set along the route. Our pilgrimage arrangements were relatively easy, staying in hotels, with our luggage being transported each day to the next stop. And the 80-mile walk was only a fraction of the most common longer one that begins in the Pyrenees and covers over 500 miles.

We were told to train for the pilgrimage by taking long walks on Block Island and in Central Park in New York. After several weeks of preparing, we thought we would be ready, except that we had not anticipated the many hills and almost daily rain. Each day, the walk began with a talk by Father George Witt, then the pastor of St. Ignatius Church, in which he gave us some points to meditate on our own while walking dur-

JOSÉ MARÍA DE LASA

ing the day, and said Mass before dinner. We were about 30 people in our group. I tended to walk among the last of the group, with María Teresa way ahead of me. The first day it took her six hours to get to the destination, while I walked for seven and a half hours. In addition to the spiritual benefits one derives from the walk, we enjoyed the opportunity to meet people from across the world and engage in meaningful conversations. María Teresa met during the walk two Korean girls and they walked together for a good while. One of the girls asked María Teresa if she was married and when she said, "yes," the girl asked, "and for how many years?" When María Teresa answered, "50 years," the girls exclaimed "50 years with one man!" What a great relief it was for me to arrive in Santiago de Compostela, having been able to complete the seven-day walk with significant spiritual rewards and only a couple of blisters on my feet. And I lost 6 lbs!

Another spiritually rewarding trip we made was a one-week pilgrimage to the Holy Land, led by Father Jim Martin, a Jesuit priest, editor-at-large of *America Magazine*, and a best-selling author of a number of books, including *Jesus: A Pilgrimage* that was inspired by his trip the prior year to the Holy Land with another Jesuit and friend. (This book is a great read.) Accompanying us on our trip with him were three other Jesuit priests, including Father Matt Malone, the magazine's president and editor-in-chief. We began the pilgrimage at the Sea of Galilee, visiting sites where Jesus lived and preached such as Capernaum, Bethsaida, Nazareth and Cana and then journeyed to Jerusalem passing through Jericho and Bethany, where so many of Jesus's miracles were performed. While in Jerusalem, which houses some of the most important sites for the three major world religions, Christianity, Judaism and Islam, we visited the Church of the Holy Sepulcher, the holiest place for Catholic and Orthodox Christians, and the site of Jesus's crucifixion, burial, and Resurrection. Before going to the Holy Sepulchre, we spent a couple of hours in Gethsemani, at the foot of the Mount of Olives in Jerusalem, where Jesus prayed and his disciples slept the night before his crucifixion. It was wonderful occasion for us to pray and meditate.

We also visited the Temple Mount in the old city of Jerusalem, a raised platform and the place where the Jewish temples stood prior to the Roman conquest. Near its center is the Dome of the Rock, an Islamic Shrine built in 691 and considered Islam's third holiest site. For Muslims, it is the site of the Prophet Muhammad's ascension into heaven. The Dome covers the Foundation Stone considered the holiest site in Judaism, as it is considered the site where Abraham prepared to sacrifice his son Isaac to God. The Western Wall is another holy site of Judaism, and it is also called the "Wailing Wall" because of the practice of Jews weeping the destruction of the temples. I also prayed at the "Western Wall," wearing a Jewish skullcap, and placed a prayer note in the wall crevices, as many visitors are encouraged to do. In the note I prayed for all of you and that you may have faith. This trip to the Holy Land was actually the second one we made. In 1983 we went there on a pilgrim-

131

age organized by Father Llorente, with group of about 15 persons. Bebé, Jose, Andrés and Mamá and Naty my sister also came along. The trip included a few other couples some of them friends of ours, and all having an affiliation with the *Agrupación Católica Universitaria.*

We much enjoyed an Ignatian pilgrimage to Spain in 2016 led by Father Matt Malone following in the footsteps of St. Ignatius, visiting Loyola, Aranzazu, Xavier, Manresa, Montserrat and Barcelona, and reliving the actions and places so often mentioned during the many Ignatian spiritual exercises we have been fortunate to attend. Before the pilgrimage began we spent a couple of days in Bilbao, visiting nearby Plentzia where grandfather Fabián was born. Then, we traveled in the Rioja province, visiting some of its fine vineyards, and enjoying the beautiful views. Following the pilgrimage, we visited the Costa Brava, close to Barcelona, in a coastal region of Catalonia in northeastern Spain, and had the pleasure of touring around, and spending time with Manuel Delgado, Jr., his wife Andrea, and their youngest son, Manolito.

In 2014, we went to Russia, first visiting Moscow, followed by a cruise along the Volga River to St. Petersburg during which we stopped in a few towns, including Uglich, founded a thousand years ago. Along the way, we visited medieval monasteries, and enjoyed the beautiful scenery filled with enormous birch trees. In Moscow we visited many interesting places beginning, of course, with Red Square and the significant buildings, including the Lenin tomb that contains for viewing Lenin's embalmed body and Saint Basil's Cathedral. Also on the large plaza is the former GUM Department Store, now filled with modern, world-renowned European shops. Presiding behind Lenin's tomb, and the tombs of other soviet leaders is the Kremlin, the former seat of the government of the Soviet Union now housing the central office of the Russian Federation. It is in the Kremlin where its president, Vladimir Putin, and other senior government officials, maintain working residences. While exploring the Red Square I kept thinking of the Cold War, its threats of nuclear war, the horrors of communism, and the nefarious influence the Soviet Union had in helping maintain the communist regime in Cuba.

We visited the underground facility in the middle of Moscow, known as "Bunker 42" or the "Cold War Museum," which was the emergency command post of the nuclear forces of the Soviet Union, with a desk reserved for Josef Stalin, the supreme leader of the country and its dictator from the mid-1920s until his death in 1953. During our visit, I somberly pondered with an eerie feeling the risk that the world faced during the Cold War, particularly during the Cuban Missile Crisis. Today, with several other countries, armed with nuclear weapons, including the unstable North Korea, we should pray that the risk of a nuclear war will never materialize. Russia regrettably remains a major nuclear power and the U.S. and Russia should indeed restore negotiations to reduce their nuclear arsenals.

Trips to Cuba in recent years have been very impactful. María Teresa made the first trip in 1998 on the occasion of the visit to Cuba of Pope Saint John Paul II. We both were invited to join a large group of people accompanying John Cardinal O'Connor, Archbishop of New York, leading a delegation to Cuba on that occasion, which contributed to improving the relationship between the Cuban government and the Catholic Church. I declined to accept the invitation given that I had been a member of the resistance before leaving Cuba and continued the struggle for a few years after my exile in the U.S. I was somewhat fearful of going on the trip given my counter-revolutionary background.

The following year we were invited to join two members of the Order of Malta in Washington on a visit sponsored by Caritas (Catholic Charities). María Teresa persuaded me to accept the invitation. At that time, I had been in touch with a senior member of the Cuban delegation, not yet an embassy, representing Cuba in Washington. He had made a few trips to Chicago to visit my niece Natalia and me, since we had been advocating for relief from the U.S. embargo on Cuba and we thus were regarded as "friends," although he was fully aware of my counter-revolutionary background. When he learned of the Order de Malta invitation, he told me that I should accept it and visit Cuba and that nothing untoward would happen to me. I told him that I would agree to go, but only if I received a letter from the head of the Cuban delegation in Washington formally inviting me to visit Cuba, and with a smile I said to him that he could infer what the consequences might be if I became subject to any reprisals. I did get the letter, and whether it played any role or not, the fact is that I faced no government obstacle during the trip.

It was a very moving trip, filled with memories of our youth, and María Teresa and I visited what had been our homes. The purpose of the trip was to visit many of the humanitarian works around the island under the sponsorship of the Order of Malta and operated through Caritas Cubana. We traveled the whole island, stopping in many cities, lodging in churches and bishop's houses, and riding in a small car that carried the four of us from the U.S., the driver, and Rolando ("Piro") Suarez, then the head of Caritas in Cuba. I very vividly recall my eyes tearing up when Piro welcomed me at the airport in Havana and said: "José María, bienvenido a tu patria" or "welcome to your motherland." The next morning we went to Mass at the well-known Convent of the Missionaries of Charity, located in front of the Parque Maceo by the seashore, which provides a home and care for severely handicapped people. There was a small band playing music during the Mass and after its conclusion a nun asked us if we wanted to have them play some traditional Cuban music. My eyes tearing up again as they began playing. On every day of our journey in Cuba we experienced sadness and happiness.

A number of other humanitarian trips have taken us to Cuba, almost yearly over the last ten years, as part of trips of small groups organized by our good friend and relative, Consuelo Aróstegui Isaacson, co-founder of Friends of Caritas Cubana (FCC), an entity founded in Boston over 20 years ago to raise funds for Caritas Cubana. Through fundraising events principally in Boston, New York and Miami, and private donations, FCC's yearly donations over the last few years have exceeded $500,000, and larger amounts in years that included fundraising to help victims of hurricanes hitting the island. María Teresa and I serve on the steering committee that helps organize the New York fundraising events. The Cuba trips led by Consuelo consist of visiting centers around the island where Caritas offers help to people in need, including, the elderly, the sick and disabled, persons living with HIV/AIDS, children and adults with Down syndrome or who are autistic, and other people who are particularly vulnerable. Those trips give us the opportunity to witness the work being done, become aware of specific needs that demand additional fundraising assistance from us, and more importantly, with our presence signify our support for all those in the Caritas staff doing the marvelous work in Cuba. That staff consists of about 80 salaried workers and over 2,000 volunteers, most of whom are trained professionals. Our contacts with them over the years are a source of inspiration and give us hope in the success of work yet to be done.

On the subject of Cuba I should mention our friendship with Father José Conrado Rodríguez, a Cuban priest who became well known in 1994 when a strongly worded letter he wrote to Fidel Castro was published outside Cuba. He has not ceased to denounce the abuses of the Cuban government and has been the most outspoken church figure in Cuba, often displeasing the church hierarchy, which has been more accommodating to the wishes of the government in an effort to obtain concessions that have permitted the church to enhance its religious practices. Fr. Conrado has been a good friend for many years. Our son Jose spent time working in his parish in the summers of 1994 and 1995, teaching English and accompanying Fr. Conrado on his daily ministries to his parishioners. Fr. Conrado joined us on Block Island for Jose and Caroline's wedding, celebrated a Mass for them, and in the following years, baptized all three of their daughters. In 2015, on the occasion of María Teresa's and my 50th wedding anniversary, he again traveled to Block Island to say a celebratory Mass and join the family in the festivities.

In 2010, in Warsaw, Poland, Fr. Conrado was given the Geremek Award in recognition of exceptional individuals who bravely commit to introducing democratic values and practices, often in unfriendly conditions. The previous award recipient had been Nelson Mandela, the famed South African leader who spent over 20 years in prison before being elected Prime Minister. The award was presented to Fr. Conrado by Madeleine Albright, Lech Walesa, and the then U.S. Secretary of State, Hillary Clinton. Jose, Carlos Saladrigas, and his wife Olga, all good friends of Fr. Conrado, accompanied him on this trip. He continues his ministries in Cuba as a parish priest in the Province of Santa Clara and travels often to the U.S. where he visits his numerous groups of friends, is often interviewed by the media, and never stops calling for changes in Cuba.

SOME NOTABLE AFFILIATIONS

I should highlight some noteworthy organizations with which I have been involved. Lauren Finnell, a friend from Larchmont, founded in 1987 The Resource Foundation (TRF), a non-profit organization, with capital of some $15,000. He had been a volunteer in the 1960s with the Peace Corps, an organization run by the U.S. government, in which volunteers, typically college students, are sent abroad to work on social and economic development projects for a period of two years. Established by President Kennedy, this program affords young Americans an opportunity to get to know other cultures. His work with the Peace Corps in Latin America inspired Loren to create TRF. For 30 years, TRF has been a leader in supporting programs in Latin America that empower individuals to improve their lives. TRF's principal activity is to obtain donations from U.S. corporations, foundations and individuals, which are channeled to charitable organizations in Latin America. These organizations become affiliates of TRF and are involved in projects dealing with, among others activities, education and job skill development, healthcare, women's empowerment, and microenterprises. I joined TRF in 1989 as a member of its board of directors and I served as chairman from 2009 to 2011. During that time, María

Teresa and I visited a number of affiliated organizations in Peru and Chile to learn more about their work and convey TRF's commitment to continue to assist their efforts. I should note that Pilar Finnell, Lauren's wife, has always played, through her support of Lauren, a key role in the success of TRF. Also noteworthy is the significant contribution, both financial and otherwise, that Larry Prince made in the founding of TRF and in the leadership role he had in the organization over many years. Lauren, Pilar, Larry, his wife, Judith, and María Teresa and I have remained good friends and we all get together from time to time.

In 2004, I joined the Cuba Study Group (CSG), an organization made up of business and professional individuals who wish to achieve a peaceful change in Cuba. I have been on its executive board since that time. Our aim is to facilitate change in Cuba and help empower individuals and promote civil society development. Our mission statement is: "To help facilitate a peaceful change in Cuba leading to a free and open society, respect for human rights and the rule of law, a productive market-based economy and the reunification of the Cuban Nation." Our principal goal has been to change U.S. policy towards Cuba.

To that effect, CSG for years has advocated for the lifting of the U.S. embargo on Cuba, which after 57 years of being in effect has failed to achieve its purpose of bringing about a free and democratic Cuba. The embargo has in fact acted as a crutch for the Cuban government, which blames the embargo for its dismal economic performance. CSG, working at times with the Council of the Americas, submitted to the White House on more than one occasion proposals detailing the actions that the President could take, without approval by Congress, to change U.S. policy towards Cuba. The actions we proposed were the ones that President Barak Obama put into effect on December 17, 2014, in a historic initiative that included the restoration of diplomatic relations, the lifting of some travel restrictions on U.S. citizens, and the expansion of U.S. trade with Cuba. The Obama opening was widely supported in the U.S., including by a majority of Cuban-Americans. Cubans enthusiastically welcomed the move.

CSG was also instrumental in the creation of the project, "Cuba Emprende" under the auspices of the Catholic Church. Its mission is to offer training and advisory services to entrepreneurs who wish to start or improve a small business in activities that have been authorized by the government. The core program consists of 80 hours of classroom instruction in the areas of marketing and management, finance and accounting, sales and customer service, and human resources. Graduates are offered continuing advisory services. Another noteworthy activity of CSG is the reconciliation project, which seeks to provide Cubans everywhere with information regarding reconciliation processes which have taken place around the world like the one that Nelson Mandela put into effect in South Africa and which was very successful. We have held three reconciliation conferences in Miami, inviting speakers who have participated in, or are knowledgeable about, these reconciliation processes. When a free and democratic Cuba is finally established we aspire to have Cubans in Cuba who might have been supporters or sympathizers of the Revolution and Cubans who suffered under it or had to abandon their country as exiles, become reconciled with each other. This is easier said than done, but it is important to embrace reconciliation as a goal.

In 2011, I joined the board of directors of the Visiting Nurse Service of New York (VNSNY). VNSNY is the largest not-for-profit home-based health care in the U.S., serving New York City, as well as Nassau, Suffolk, and Westchester Counties. On any given day, VNSNY has over 30,000 patients in its care. I serve on its Governance Committee and also on the board of directors of its Hospice and Palliative Care branch. Four years ago, after a few weeks of training, I began to volunteer at a hospice residence located near our apartment in New York, where I go work one day every week on a two-hour shift. Hospice care is designed to support people during their final phase of life and is provided in most cases at their own homes, with some patients cared for in nursing homes and at hospice centers such as the residence where I volunteer.

To qualify for hospice care under Medicaid and Medicare, the person needs to have been certified by a physician as likely having six months or less to live. Volunteers in hospice care include people from a variety of work backgrounds and life experiences, such as landscapers and grounds keepers, barbers, beauticians, and musicians. Most of the volunteers are involved in providing comfort and peace to the patient and family during the end of life. What I do consists principally in just sitting down with the patient in his or her room, engaging in conversation, caressing a hand or an arm, helping the person eat or drink, calling a nurse for assistance, or just watching a TV program together, and always smiling. At first I thought that being with dying people would be stressful and sad, but in fact I have seen many smiles from them and they have inspired me. Remember, you always receive more than you give when helping others.

It is my hope that I have conveyed that not only faith, but perseverance, endurance, acceptance of failures and disappointments, rectification of errors, commitment to marriage, enjoyment of family and friends, service to others, and hope, are themes from my life. With the grace of God, I have tried to live by these guiding principles, albeit in an imperfect way.

I want to end my memoirs by telling you that as much as I have loved Cuba and will continue to help that country in whatever way I can, I am indebted to the United States of America, another country I love, the one that welcomed me, where I received a wonderful education, developed a successful career, and where you all have been raised. I believe that I have lived the American Dream.

PHOTOS

My father Miguel and mother Conchita, 1933.

Havana Yacht Club, 1944. Adults from left: My father, grandfather José María, grandfather Fabián, my mother, Tía Bebita. Children from left: The Author, Miguel, Naty, Elena.

My house in Havana.

At the country home of Cuba's president Mario García Menocal, sitting at left. The famed Italian tenor Enrico Caruso is sitting in front of him. My grandfather José María is standing in the back in the white suit. Photo taken during Menocal's presidency, 1917-1922.

Our wedding in the Church of the Little Flower in Coral Gables, Florida,
on November 23, 1963.

Naty with uncle José María, Larchmont, 1996.

Elena, in Chunchon, where the demilitarized buffer zone between
North Korea and South Korea is located, 1963.

In New Haven home, 1972. From left: The Author, mother, Miguel, Elena, Naty.

In 1986, with our children on Block Island, where we spent many summers vacationing. Some of our most cherished family memories come from Block Island.

Boston, 2017. From left: Edward, Elena, Ana Maria, Maria Teresa (Bebe), Sofia, Richard.

Boulder, Colorado, 2017. From left: Lola, Jose, Tesa, Daisy, Caroline.

Flint Park, Larchmont, 2017. From left: Andres, Gabriel, Oscar, Kyle, Sebastian.

Thanksgiving, Larchmont, 2016. Carlos and Caroline Claire with
(from left to right) Halle, Marinna, Camile.

Christmas, 2017, at our apartment in New York. Naty with daughters, grandchildren, great grandchildren, sons-in-law, boyfriends and girlfriend of grandchildren.

Lima, Perú, 1992. Miguel with his children and grandchildren.

Summer, 2017. Figueroa family reunion in Virgen Gorda, Virgin Islands.

Block Island, 2013, during the celebration of our 50th wedding anniverasary.
From left: The Author, Javier, María Teresa, Sylvia, Fr. José Conrado Rodríguez.

Amando Llorente S.J.
Father Llorente was the Director of the Agrupacion Catolica Universitaria (ACU)
from 1952 until his death in 1910. He married us and was our spiritual director.

PT Boat at training camp on Catalina Island, Dominican Republic, 1964. When armed it had a 20mm cannon set in the stern and three 50 caliber machine guns - one in the bow and one in starboard and port, respectively.

28-ft Bertram, named "Juanin", used in infiltrations into Cuba and the attack on the Hotel Rosita de Hornedo, in 1962, using a 20mm cannon set in the stern.

The Author and Miguel at the training camp on the Catalina Island,
Dominican Republic, 1964.

DRE reunion celebrating Miguel's 70th Anniversary (2005). From left:
Juan Manuel Salvat, Alberto Muller, Bernabé Peña, José Antonio González Lanuza,
Miguel de Lasa, Miguel García Armengol, Isidro Borjas, Luis
Fernández Rocha, Fernando García Chacón and The Author.

In the chapel of Belen Jesuit Preparatory School, in Miami, Florida, 2016.
From left: Ernesto Fernández Travieso, S.J., July Hernández,
Bernabé Peña, The Author and José Antonio González Lanuza.
Travieso, Hernández and G. Lanuza are the three DRE members
who infiltrated into Cuba at Punto Enrique.

Meeting with the Dalai Lama, in his home in Dharamshala, India.
From left: Roger Thomas, Tica, The Author,
Dalai Lama, Sava Thomas, María Teresa.

Treasure Cay, Bahamas, 1998. From left: Betty and Carlos García-Vélez, Zoila Margarita and Fernando García Chacón, María Teresa and the Author, Manuel and Rosario Delgado.

Block Island, 2000, with old friends from the time I began my career at the Cleary Gottlieb law firm in New York. From left: Jim Beery, The Author, Jim Munsell, Roger Thomas.